The Entrepreneur's Guide to Understanding Angel and Venture Investing

By
Jude Conway

"The Entrepreneur's Guide to Understanding Angel and Venture Investing," by Jude Conway. ISBN 978-1-60264-712-1.

Published 2011 by Virtualbookworm.com Publishing Inc., P.O. Box 9949, College Station, TX 77842, US. ©2011, Jude Conway. All rights reserved. No part of this publication may be reproduced, stored in a retrieval system, or transmitted in any form or by any means, electronic, mechanical, recording or otherwise, without the prior written permission of Jude Conway.

Manufactured in the United States of America.

TABLE OF CONTENTS

INTRODUCTION

Possibly the most misunderstood sector of the financial markets is seed stage to early stage equity investing. Unlike bank financing or the public equity markets, relatively few people attempting to access early stage equity financing know much about it. Many people beginning businesses today have heard of angel and venture capitalists and believe that they are the solution to their financial woes. They may have read an article about someone receiving capital from these sources or a friend has suggested that they need to obtain venture capital financing, but they know little more than that.

Even more problematic is that many, if not most small business counselors, coaches and advisors know little about how venture capital and angel investing works. It is amazing to me, having been involved in early stage investing for over twenty years, how many people confuse it as a form of lending, or even worse as some sort of grant that doesn't need to be paid back.

In the chapters that follow I will explain exactly what venture capital and angel investing are, how they work, what businesses are appropriate for this kind of investing and why. I will also explain how early stage investors value a company along with the typical process that a company must go through to obtain such capital. I will attempt to do this in layperson terms that can be understood by most small business owners.

I will describe the different early stages of a company's development as defined by the investing community.

I will limit the discussion in this book to seed, start-up and early stage investing, not because venture capitalists and angels only invest in these stages because they don't. In fact most of their investing may be in the expansion stage. I limit it to these stages because entrepreneurs that get beyond these stages better understand their financing options and how they work.

The early chapters may seem too elementary for some but I have learned through the years that many people getting into business need a basic finance primer. This book is meant to be read in its entirety to get a full understanding of early stage investing, but it is my hope that it will also be used as a reference or guide when someone has a question about a specific topic.

This book is not meant to be used by those with equity finance experience or for MBA candidates wishing to better understand the intricacies of the industry. Instead it is meant for those businesses and their professional advisors that are trying to determine whether angel or venture capital financing is appropriate for their situation.

Although early stage equity investing is a form of private equity investing, I will attempt to avoid using this term. In the capital markets, "private equity" is a separate class of investing that generally implies later stage equity financing in much larger dollar amounts than what early stage businesses can expect.

1.

WHAT ARE SEED, START-UP AND EARLY STAGE EQUITY?

One of the things I find interesting is the apparent mystery surrounding private (not publicly traded) equity markets by the small business community. I have a presentation that I have given to entrepreneurs entitled "De-Mystifying Angel and Venture Capital Investing." Once when being interviewed for a news article regarding my presentation I was quoted as follows:

"Most people's eyes glaze over when venture capital or angel investing is mentioned. They feel it's somewhere between Voodoo and quantum physics. While the details of an angel or venture capital deal can get quite complicated the basic concept is quite simple. It's when someone other than friends or family purchase shares in your company. Once entrepreneurs understand how this works, they can make an informed decision whether or not to pursue this type of financing."

While this may not be the best way to describe privately held equity, it does define it in lay person terms because most people understand the concept of shares of stock. This allows them to stop thinking it is some sort of usurious debt obligation or even worse a grant of some kind.

In the quote above I was only speaking of angel and venture capital; for our purposes since we are talking about all investors, the words, "other than friends and family" would be deleted from the definition and we should add something about the company being privately held. Following is an easily understood definition of privately held equity:

Privately held equity is shares of stock that are owned by someone in a business when the stock from that business is not traded on a stock exchange or over the counter (with some notable exceptions, virtually all stock purchased in the seed to early stages of a business is privately held).

So the equity portion of the phrase "seed to early stage equity" has been defined. Now it's time to define what is meant by seed to early stage. This can be quite confusing because the general public's definition of terms such as seed, start-up and early stage can be quite different than that of the investing community. For instance, to investors the start up stage is not when the business first starts and early stage is really the third or fourth stage in a business' life cycle. So what are the definitions?

Seed Stage – The earliest stage of development in a company's life cycle when

the product or service is at the concept through research and development phases of a business (many in the investing community divide this phase into two phases - pre-seed and seed).

Start-up – In investing terms, the stage in a company's life cycle when it is ready to generate product revenue. Another way of saying this is, when a company has a product that is ready to enter the market or to be sold. In most companies, especially technology companies, this is not the same as the starting date of the company's operations.

Early Stage – The stage in a business' life cycle after it has sales revenue but generally before there is positive cash flow and/or profitability.

You should be aware that there are certainly other stages in a business' life cycle that are financed privately and even financed by angel and venture capital but these companies are more likely to have the sophistication to better understand the private equity markets or the wherewithal to retain someone that does, so this book will concentrate on the these three earliest stages. Now that we have private equity defined and seed, start-up and early stage defined, we are ready to combine the definitions into one.

Seed to Early Stage Equity – **Shares of privately held stock in a business that is in the earliest stages of a business' life cycle from pre-seed or seed stage, through the**

5

start-up stage and into the early stage. Another way of saying this would be shares of privately held stock in a business that is in the earliest stages of business' life cycle from concept phase through the point at which it has positive cash flow and/or has reached profitability.

2.

WHO INVESTS IN SEED TO EARLY STAGE BUSINESS?

Friends, family, angel investors and venture capital funds invest in the earliest stages of business. But do all of them invest in all of these stages? No, generally they do not.

Figure 1 shows that the earliest investing Is done by friends and family, followed by angels and then venture capital. The reasons for this continuum are many. It has to do in large part on risk of the investment, the length of time an investor wishes to hold any single investment, alternative investments that an investor may have available to him or her and the return on those alternative investments. In the case of friends and family the reasons for the investment may even be other than financial. Later I will go over in greater detail all of these reasons.

I will mention that that "friends and family" generally do not have the wherewithal or the opportunity to invest in any but the earliest stages of a company's development. Angel investors do not necessarily need to invest in the concept or seed stages but by the time a company reaches expansion stage the amount of money needed is usually greater than angels can supply.

Venture capital firms invest where risk and reward are optimal. Their investors have the greatest flexibility when it comes to alternative investments and the venture capital firms have large amounts of capital. This allows them to invest later than angels while taking much less risk and getting comparable returns.

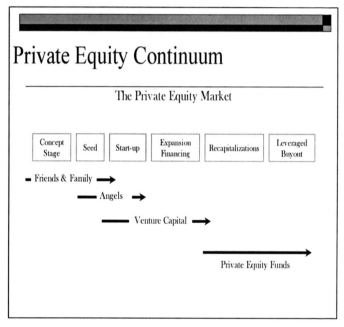

Figure 1 – Private Equity Continuum – Which private equity investors typically fund each of the early stages of a company's development.

There is another concept that is not included in this continuum and that is the concept of bootstrapping. This is the practice of self financing a business by whatever means is available, such as maxing out credit cards, selling one's car or getting a second home mortgage.

Bootstrapping generally occurs when no other financing is available during the concept and seed stages and may replace friends and family or supplement it.

So as Figure 1 implies, during the concept stage you are on your own, tapping into savings, selling off assets, running up credit card balances and asking (sometimes begging) your best friends or parents for a loan or to have enough faith in you to take a piece of the company (equity) for money to get you through the difficult times.

When you look at Figure 1 you may ask why it shows angel and venture money coming along during the seed stage of development. The reason for this is that some angels will invest in this stage and few but some venture funds are interested in seed level investing. However, the frequency of this especially with venture capital firms is rare and is generally limited to pharmaceutical products and other very high tech endeavors where the returns are potentially high and the investor can sell the investment well before the company reaches a positive cash flow or profitability.

It is more likely that friends and family will be investors in the concept and seed stages with the possibility of some government grants and loans during product development. Angel investors may start to get interested at this stage if a prototype has been built and all that remains is product and market testing. Most angel investors would still prefer to wait to invest in the start-up stage when they can see the product and know it works.

Venture capital firms will generally wait to invest in companies that have sold product in the market. While angels may be satisfied that the product can be built and works, venture funds generally want to know that it can be built, it works and that a significant number of people are willing to buy it. As can be seen in Figure 2, the venture capital investments continue to move to Later stage deals. In 1995, thirty-eight percent of the venture money went to seed, start-up or early stage businesses. In 2007, only twenty-two percent of the money went into the same categories. The year 2007 is used in this table because it was the last full year of venture investing prior to the venture industry collapse that began in late 2008.

Does all of this mean that if your business survives the seed and start-up stages that you have a good chance of receiving angel or venture financing to get your product to market or bridge the financial gap until you have positive cash flow? No, just because your company has reached the stage that may attract an angel investor or even venture capital it does not mean that it is a fit for an investment by either one of them. Even if it is a fit it may not be something you wish to pursue. In the next chapter we'll take a look at the definitions for angels and venture capitalists and what companies are attractive investments for them. Later we will look at whether you as an

entrepreneur wish to pursue institutional equity
financing.

Then and Now Venture Capital Investments by Dollars

1995		2007	
Startup/ Seed	16.0%	Startup/Seed	4.0%
Early Stage	22.0%	Early Stage	18.0%
Expansion	46.0%	Expansion	37.0%
Later Stage	16.0%	Later Stage	41.0%

**Figure 2 – Then and Now Venture Capital Investment
by Dollars, a comparison of 1995 and 2007.**

3

WHO ARE THESE ANGELS AND WHAT IS VENTURE CAPITAL?

We've defined seed to early stage equity, talked a little about who might invest in each stage of a company's early development but we've yet to define what distinguishes a family member from an angel or an angel from a venture capitalist. So let's do that now.

"Friends and Family" is a term used for people the entrepreneur knows and that invest in a business at least partly due to the personal relationship with that entrepreneur. It doesn't necessarily need to be a friend or family. It could be the person that has serviced your car for the past ten years or your doctor, dentist or insurance agent. Due to securities regulations it is advisable that one has more than a Passing acquaintance with anyone investing in one's company. One may hear this group sarcastically referred to this group sarcastically referred to as "the three F's – Friends, Family and Fools."

"Friends and Family" may invest in your company because they know and trust your judgment, passion, work ethic and character. It may be that you're in a difficult situation, such as being chronically unemployed or underemployed and feel you need their support to make a positive change in your life. It might be that they just think your business idea is the best thing since sliced bread and don't want to miss a chance of a lifetime. After all, they may not have the opportunity to invest in something like this often.

"Friends and Family" may be, but most likely are not sophisticated investors or what the industry and the Security and Exchange Commission refer to as accredited investors. An accredited investor in layperson terms is someone who is wealthy enough that they can afford to lose their investment without affecting the way in which they live. The legal definition changes periodically and so anyone needing to know the legal definition should consult with an attorney or investment advisor for the current definition.

Now that we know what is meant by "Friend and Family" lets move on to Angels or Angel Investors. Really there are three types of angel investing, all involve angel investors. The first is an angel investor investing on his or her own. Second, there are angel investors that invest as part of an "Angel Network". Finally, there are funds, referred to as "Angel Funds" whose investors are a group of angels.

Angel Investor(s) – A Wealthy individual or group of individuals (usually accredited investors) that regularly invest in entrepreneurial companies. Amount of investment may range from $25,000 to $1 million plus.

Angel Network – A Group of angel investors that work together to hear investment presentations, review deals, conduct due diligence and make investments.

Unlike an angel fund investors in an angel network make investments as individual investors instead of as one fund investment. In many angel networks, this mechanism allows the investor to decide whether or not to invest in each individual deal, regardless of what others in the network might do.

Angel Funds – An investment fund capitalized by a group of angel investors that makes investments in entrepreneurial companies as one investor. Since all the money in an angel Fund is pooled up front when an investment is made it is made as a fund. Once a decision is made to invest, the fund invests a pro rata share of each investor's total committed investment. The individual investor does not have the ability to pass on the investment in which the fund has decided to invest.

An angel fund may be professionally managed by someone that is not an angel investor in the fund or managed by a group of the angel investors of that fund. Angel funds tend to be regional in scope investing in a metropolitan area, multi-county area or statewide. Most do not invest beyond about a 100 mile radius of its office.

So the common thread to the three types of angel investing is that individual angel investors are involved in all of them. It is the way that they are involved that differs.

Venture capital funds are similar to angel funds except the investors tend to be institutional investors instead of individuals and the funds are in all cases professionally managed. Let's take a look at a definition for Venture Capital.

Venture Capital Fund – A professionally managed fund raised primarily from institutional investors; e.g. pension funds, banks, foundations and university endowments. Nearly all venture capital funds are organized as limited partnerships with a ten year life. Venture capital is invested in the form of equity, usually preferred stock, in privately held companies at various stages of development.

Venture capital funds are usually much bigger than angel funds but small venture funds can be similar in size to large angel Funds, perhaps in the twenty to twenty five million dollar range. These small venture funds may have a combination of angel investors and institutional investors in their funds. Angel funds may be as small as $1 million dollars but most are at least $5 million. Venture capital funds may be $20 million dollars or even less but most purely venture funds are fifty million to multi billion dollar funds.

I have provided definitions for the types of early stage investors. Some may argue over a specific word or phrase in these definitions or may have a definition they prefer but I believe that most people that are involved in the industry would agree that these definitions capture the essence of who these investors are and how they operate.

Knowing the difference between the types of investors is useful for several reasons. It allows one to know what another is talking about when they mention one of these terms. It also helps to understand why each type of investor does what they do when making an investment.

The definitions are useful but they do not go far enough if what you really need to know is whether they will invest or how much might they invest in a particular business. So let's take a look at some of these questions so that you might better understand what fits for your particular situation.

You are on your own when it comes to "Friends and Family". You really need to strike the right chord with these people and since you will know these people before you approach them, you know better than I what might work. One piece of advice however, especially outside your immediate family is to approach people that might understand and have an interest in your product. If it's a new fuel system for an automobile, it might be the local car dealer or auto repair shop, if it's a retail concept it might be the owner of a store that you frequent and if it's a piece of new medical technology it might be your physician.

Also remember that these people are likely to be relatively small investors, anywhere from the first $1,000 to get your business incorporated and business cards printed to $50,000-$100,000 to fund some product development or purchase needed equipment. Many times the return they are looking for is there money back at some point in the future, especially immediate family. Others may want a bit more of a return but are also looking for the satisfaction of helping someone they know succeed in business and life.

Angel investors invest in businesses relatively close to home, say within 100 miles. They are probably interested in particular industries or technologies. Those that are successful entrepreneurs themselves are likely to invest in the industry where they succeeded or something closely related.

Many times angels are looking for a way to stay involved but not full time. They may wish to provide advise to the company; act as an interim Chief Executive Officer (CEO), Chief Financial Officer (CFO) or Chief Operating Officer (COO); or perhaps serve on the company's board of directors, perhaps as chairman. Do not discount this type of advice it can be invaluable. Just make sure that your personality fits with theirs and that they will listen as well as provide advice.

As was mentioned earlier angel investors may invest anywhere from $10,000 to $1 million. Angel networks are just a group of angels that look at deals together. What an angel network does bring to the table is the ability to reach several angels at once, the possibility that a member of the group maybe knowledgeable of your technology or industry and may sway others to invest, the likelihood that one person will be assigned as your advisor and mentor and as a representative on your board and finally the ability to aggregate the investments of several angels together into what looks more like one much larger investment than several small ones.

An angel network is still likely to stay close to home. Remember most are regional in scope. The investment size may be from $50,000 to well over $1 million depending on how many in the network decide to invest in your deal.

Angel Funds will be much more structured than individual angel investors or angel networks. This is primarily due to the fact that the angel investors are entrusting their money to someone else up front, without the benefit of being able to decide whether or not to invest in each individual deal. This type of investment vehicle is referred to as a "blind pool" as opposed to say a mutual fund where an individual can see the investments currently in a fund where they plan to invest.

Because they are investing in a blind pool, the angels need to be confident ahead of time that those investing the money know what the angels are looking for in the investment. Generally this means the fund will have an investment policy that will state the geographical boundaries of investments, the industries in which investments will or will not be made, the minimum and maximum size of investments and which stages of company development investments will or will not be made.

In some ways an angel fund can be easier for the entrepreneur to work with because you know up front where they make investments. If your business needs less than its minimum or is not in the right geographical area there is no need to pursue an investment from them. On the flip side, if you do fit all their criteria your odds may be enhanced and you may wish to target them.

Angel funds, if well run will set their minimums and maximums based on the total size of the fund. A fund needs to have a minimum number of investments in order to be able to diversify its portfolio but does not want too many investments because it is more than the management team can effectively manage. Two general rules of thumb is that a fund should not put more than 10%-15% of its total funds in any single investment and that generally a fund is looking at making somewhere in the neighborhood of 15-25 investments throughout the life of the fund.

Given these rules of thumb one can take a look at the total fund size and determine whether or not an investment is out the funds range. I should also mention that the 10%-15% rule is not how much the fund should put into the initial investment but how much they will invest over the life of the investment. Most funds reserve money for at least two additional rounds of investment. The amount and number of rounds that are reserved for depends on the stage and size of the deal.

This means only, that a $5 million angel fund is unlikely to initially invest a million dollars in your company. Likewise, a $100 million venture fund will not invest $50,000 in a business. Neither of these investments is financially responsible given the size of the particular funds.

There are many similarities between how venture capital funds and angel funds operate but there are probably just as many differences. A venture fund is similar to an angel fund in that the investors are investing in a blind pool therefore the fund will have an investment policy with similar characteristics. Also, it will more or less follow the same two general rules of thumb for setting its minimum and maximum investments.

Because the size of the investments tend to be a degree of magnitude larger in venture capital funds than they are in an angel fund and the investors tend to be more sophisticated, the investment policies, fund operations and reporting requirement become more detailed.

Size also has its benefits however. A large venture fund will likely be much less restrictive geographically for instance and may have the ability to fund your investment to profitability without need of partners in the deal. As was mentioned before venture funds tend to invest in later stage deals than do angels and angel funds. They also tend to be much more specific in the industry or industries in which they invest. For this reason they have a great deal of knowledge and expertise in given fields. If a venture fund invests in only one industry, say life sciences or information technology, they may know the industry and market much better than the entrepreneur seeking funds.

From this point forward there probably is not a great deal more to say about the investment habits of "Friends and Family" because the investments are as varied as the investors, they are comparatively informal compared to angels, angel networks or venture capital funds and they may be made for strategic, emotional and financial reasons.

Before I move on I should also mention one other type of investor or investment and that is the corporate/strategic investor. This is generally another business that will invest in a business because there is a strategic or business reason for the investment. This could be someone who supplies the entrepreneur with raw material, it could be a customer or it could be someone that is not a direct competitor but That has a product that is complementary to the entrepreneur's and is sold into the same or similar markets.

I am not discussing the corporate or strategic investor in any detail because it is fairly uncommon to see these investors at the earliest stages of a company's life cycle and the way they invest can be almost as varied as those in the "Friends and Family" category Finally, it is something that needs to be carefully analyzed on a "one on one" basis. I mention it only because it comes up from time to time. In many cases, these strategic investors can be a subset of "friends and family" because many times you know who they are and, you have worked with them in the past and they have a reason to invest that is not strictly financial.

The distinguishing characteristics of angels, angel funds and venture capital funds have now been identified. We know what size investments are common, how far from home they may travel and what stage of development interests them. But what are the odds of getting funded, how long does the process take and how do they decide which deal to fund among those that fit their minimum investment policy thresholds?

First of all the odds of getting funded depends on what type of business you have. The larger the market and the higher the profit margin the better the chances. That said, the odds are better that a particular company will not be funded. There is little knowledge about what the odds are of getting funded by an angel, angel network or even an angel fund but suffice it to say the odds are not as good as those of getting a commercial loan from a bank. The odds of being funded by a venture fund are in all likelihood, less than that of angel sources.

What we know is that venture capital funds that report data to the "Money Tree" survey taken quarterly invest in about 1%-3% of the proposals that they receive. This does not mean that only 1% to 3% of the deals get venture capital funding however, because most proposals are sent to more than one fund. The odds increase, depending on how many funds see the average deal. It should also be mentioned that many proposals are sent to funds when they do not meet the investment criteria of those funds. When I was at Hopewell Ventures, L.P. in Chicago we estimated that approximately 40% of the proposals we received did not meet our published, minimum criteria.

I will discuss why the odds are what they are, how to enhance ones odds and how the review process works in the next chapter.

4.

Is My Business Right for an Angel or Venture Capital Investment?

Figure 3 provides a list of attributes that businesses need to attract outside equity. When speaking to entrepreneurs about this list I make sure to tell them that it may not be necessary to meet all six of the items on the list below but you better be able to meet most of them. The more you meet the better and if you are going after venture capital money as opposed to angel money meeting all six may be required.

Early stage equity investors, especially angel funds and venture capital funds must make a relatively high return on the money invested because of the risk involved in the investments. High net worth individuals, like angels and institutional investors that invest in venture capital funds have many types of investment opportunities for their money. They can invest in government guaranteed bonds and certificates of deposit with low risk and low returns, corporate bonds, the stock market or certain real estate investments with medium risk and medium returns. Finally, they can accept a high risk in more speculative investments for potential high returns. Early stage equity investing fall into this speculative category along with a number of other types of investments.

What Businesses Can Attract Outside Equity (Angel or Venture Capital)?

- ❑ Ones with significant Barriers to Entry
- ❑ Ones that solve a critical problem
- ❑ Ones with high margins
- ❑ Fast Growth Companies
- ❑ Ones that are scalable
- ❑ Ones in Industries with relatively large markets

Figure 3 – What Businesses Can Attract Angel or Venture Capital?

Most investors will have a portfolio balanced with some investments in a number of different asset classes to diversify its portfolio. Angel investors may put a small amount in the riskier classes such as early stage investments but if the return is not adequate they may find other speculative investments to invest in such as oil and gas exploration, speculative real estate or low grade corporate bonds.

Venture capital funds only invest in high risk investments but as indicated earlier they are investing for a group of institutional investors that have a myriad of places to invest funds. In fact, these institutional investors put only a tiny fraction of funds in venture capital.

Here's an example that may be a bit unrealistic but illustrates why an investment in a start-up company must get a much better return than one that is traded publicly. John Doe can invest in Microsoft stock with an expected long term internal rate of return of 10% or Joe's Corner Pizza that opened last week with the same 10% internal rate of return. Joe's Corner Pizza is considered to be 100 times less likely to reach the 10% return as Microsoft. Which investment should John Doe make? It's quite obvious he should invest in Microsoft.

However, if John can get a 50% return on Joe's Pizza and only a 5% return on Microsoft and the Microsoft investment is only 8 times safer then John has a decision to make. Does he take safety over return or does he risk his money for potentially a huge payoff? If you are a large institutional investor you can make both investments and hedge your bet.

The way angel investors and venture capitalists determine what return they might be able to expect from a privately held company is to value it based on its revenue and profit margins or cash flow at some specific point in the future usually three to seven years from the time of the investment, the most typical being five years.

The reason that venture capitalists look at a three to seven year period to value deals has to do with how venture capital funds are structured. As was mentioned earlier, venture capital funds are usually structured as limited partnerships. Limited partnerships have a stated life. At the end of the life of the partnership the fund manager must liquidate investments and pay the investors their share of the proceeds. Almost all limited partnerships in the venture capital industry have a life of ten years which may be able to be extended one or two years beyond the stated life under certain circumstances. This means that venture capitalist must make investments, hold those investments for some period and sell the investments within a ten year period.

Figure 4 shows during which years a typical venture capital fund performs which activities. Generally, a venture capital firm will attempt to raise a new venture capital fund every three to five years so that they can make new investments on a continuous basis.

Given these parameters the company must grow quickly because the investor needs to be able sell his investment in that three to seven year period. If the company is growing slowly the expected return may happen too late for the investor to take advantage, besides the longer the investment is held the higher the value of the company must be in order to receive the expected return. This is based on the time/value of money.

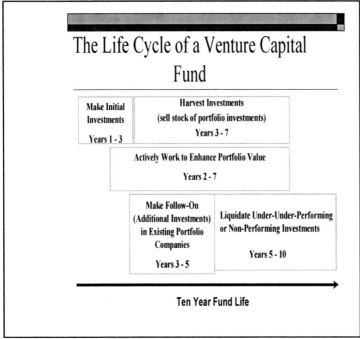

Figure 4 – The Life Cycle of a Venture Capital Fund

The market that the company is selling product into must also be relatively large in order to reach the revenues needed to obtain the expected return. Margins must also be high because a company that sells a great deal of product but makes little on each sale is worth much less than one that makes a great deal of profit on each transaction. Margins are highest in companies that have a product that is critically needed in the market place.

A large market is not enough if the business is not scalable. MerriamWebster.com defines scalable as capable of being easily expanded or upgraded on demand. What this means in business terms is that the business' product or service can be produced over and over again without the same amount of resources it took to produce the first one. For instance, to produce the first unit of a new software offering might cost millions of dollars but each one after that may be just pennies.

A good example of a product or service that is not particularly scalable is a consulting business. Each engagement by a consulting firm requires that an individual consultant or a group of consultants be assigned to it. Every piece of business of similar scope requires the same amount of time and attention as the one before. The consulting market is huge. There are millions of different types of consultants making a great living but it is not something that is likely to interest an outside investor because there are no real economies of scale.

High barrier to entry is mentioned as another critical factor in an early stage investor's decision. A barrier to entry is something that keeps competitors from entering the market. Examples of this are patents, copyrights, a secret recipe or possibly government approval or licensing. The fewer competitors one has the more product one can sell at higher prices or margins. This increases the company's profitability and thus its stock value.

Relatively few businesses can meet the requirements of both fast growth and high margins necessary to attract early stage outside equity. That does not mean that these businesses will fail or that they cannot be successful. It only means they must find other ways to obtain financing. Some of these more run of the mill businesses may have a much easier time obtaining traditional loans than the fast growth high margin businesses because while the return might be lower the risk is also significantly lower.

Innovation plays a key role in a company's ability to grow quickly and command high margins. Businesses that are not innovative find themselves more or less "commodity" products that can be or are sold by dozens if not hundreds of competitors. This leads to slow growth and small margins.

Many entrepreneurs and investors confuse innovation with high technology. While technology companies by definition are innovative. Companies can be innovative without having a high tech product. The innovation may be in the way a product is packaged, sold, serviced or distributed.

A great example of innovation that is low tech is the natural and organic food products industry. It has been growing rapidly in recent years and venture companies are investing in it. In many ways, the products they are supplanting are the high tech ones that use genetically modified grains. The manure used to fertilize these crops is replacing highly complex chemical fertilizers. The organic products industry is actually reverting to pre-technology practices but at the same time finding new ways of filling a critical need for a large percentage of today's consumers.

Another fairly low tech industry that has skyrocketed in the past decade is the bottled water industry. In its infancy all it was doing was bottling water from municipal water supplies. Some of the enhanced water found today involves more technology but the largest sector from a volume perspective is still very low tech.

How fast is "fast growth? One good rule of thumb is, a business must be able to at least double its revenue year to year for a period of three to five years. Of course if sales are starting out near zero in year one, it needs to do much better than double in sales the first two or three years.

How high is "high margins? This question is a bit more complicated. It depends on the industry, the revenue volume of the company and the product's strategic value to the buyer Suffice it to say that the "earnings before interest, taxes, depreciation and amortization" (EbITDA) once the business has scaled up generally cannot be in the low single digits as a percentage of revenue. There may be a few exceptions to this especially in consumer brand products, where market penetration may be more important than profitability.

Let's say your business is an early stage company that is generating some product revenue in a large market. You project growing revenues at a rapid rate with an estimated EbITDA of 15%. Is it a shoe-in for equity financing by angel or VC investors or is there more?

Of course, there is more. This just gets your proposal a serious look from investors. First of all the investor is not going take your word for the market, they will look into it themselves. Secondly, they will want to make sure your product is what you represent, that the advantages over the competition are real, that it is positioned correctly in the marketplace and that you are using the optimal sales channel to get your product into the market.

The investor will comb over the financial projections, challenging assumptions for sales, cost of goods sold, expenses, margins, workforce and etc. They will cut the revenue and margin projections accordingly and base their valuation on their numbers, not the company's.

Most importantly, they will evaluate management. In real estate, the three most important factors are location, location, location. In venture capital the three most important factors are management, management,

management. A friend of mine in the industry, George Lipper likes to say, "I will always take a mediocre product and a superior management team over a mediocre management team and superior product." The truth is that angel and venture capitalists will not invest unless they believe they have a superior management team and a superior product.

The reason for such importance being placed on the management team is decades of experience dealing with management teams that can not execute on the business' plan. No matter how big the market or how good the product, problems arise almost daily in a young company that can spell disaster. How the management team responds and how well they communicate with their investors will make or break a company. Figure 5 is something I have used in a number of presentations to illustrate what traits investors look for in management.

This is a very simplified description of what factors are important to early stage investors that hopefully will help you decide whether your particular business might be right for them. It is important that you know these factors so that you can decide early in the process of financing your business whether equity financing is a possibility or whether you should go a different direction, such as commercial lending. It is also important that you understand these factors, so that later when terms of an investment are discussed you understand the investor's rationale.

Investor's Expectations From Management

- Relevant Experience
- Complement each others strengths
- Past Success
- Flexibility
- Work well together
- Work Hard
- Work Intelligently
- Work Truthfully
- Work Creatively
- Work Well Under Pressure
- Communicate well to Team and Investors

Figure 5 – Investor's Expectations from Management

5.

How Do I Apply For An Equity Investment?

We are dealing with an unregulated industry with many different types of players so the process to get to an investment decision will differ somewhat on a case by case basis. Most investors however, will follow a similar process starting with a cursory review and ending with a closing.

Before we get to what the process is for the investor we will take a look at what the entrepreneur should prepare prior to requesting funds. Figure 6 lists items that a company should minimally have prepared before seeking funds. Let's take a look at each of them in more detail.

There is no legal way for an angel or venture capital firm to invest in a single proprietorship or traditional partnership. Your company must be incorporated in some way. Venture capital firms usually prefer that the company be organized as "C" corporation as opposed to a sub-chapter "S" corporation or an LLC because the venture firm usually has no way to benefit from the tax pass through benefits of these entities. An angel investor may actually prefer an LLC to a "C" corporation.

What You Need First

- ☐ Legally organized as a corporation or Limited Liability Company
- ☐ A well written business plan (this does not mean long)
- ☐ Defensible and detailed Financial Forecasts
- ☐ Ability to briefly (3-5 minutes) explain your business in easily understood terminology
- ☐ 15 – 20 minute power point presentation

Figure 6 – What You Need First. Items that should be developed before approaching an early stage investor.

Terms for different types of corporate structures are ones commonly found in the U.S. There may be different ones in other countries or there may be similar structures that have different names.

Do not panic if you find you have the wrong corporate structure. Generally you can convert from one structure to another without too much difficulty. In certain circumstances, however there could be detrimental tax consequences to the business or shareholders.

Legally organized corporate entity means more than just incorporating the business. It means having articles of incorporation and bylaws that the company follows. It means have minutes or records of each board of directors and shareholders meeting and having a "Certificate of Good Standing" in each state that you conduct business. If all of these items are not in order a businesses should try to put them in order during the time that the investor is performing its initial review and analysis.

A well written business plan is a must if seeking institutional financing of any kind. First of all it provides a document where the prospective investor can find enough information in one place to make its initial review. Just as important, it shows the investor that the company has thought through all major aspects of the business and has a strategy or "roadmap" for the business. The business plan needs to be organized, comprehensive and well written without being too long. It needs to have a one to three page executive summary, along with sections on management, the product(s), the market and competition, sales and marketing and operations. Early in the plan you need to state the problem the company is attempting to solve, how big the problem is and how the company plans to solve it.

Venture capital firms look at hundreds of deals a year and do not have time to wade through volumes of product spec sheets, letters of endorsement and scientific or technical data, at least not at the beginning of the process. They will also get fatigued if the narrative of the plan drones on about particular aspects of the business without getting to the point. Get the major points across as succinctly as possible. Finally, include a summary of the financial information towards the end of the plan and explain the finance package that is being requested. Not just the part the VC or angel is to finance but bank financing, other investors in the deal or grants that are anticipated.

The potential investor may not wade through volumes of financial projections at the beginning of the review process but will eventually analyze the financial projections with a fine tooth comb. If what you submit in summary detail at the beginning of the review process does not match what is provided later in the process, red flags will go up. Besides, it's necessary to have detailed financial projections to know how you want to proceed with operations, sales and other aspects the business that must be addressed in the body of the business plan. It is best if these projections are complete at the time of application to an investor.

Detailed financial projections, means that you have thought through and included how and when sales will occur and who the customers will be, all major costs and expenses and when they will occur and all payroll expenses and the timing of each new hire. Cash flow statement, P&L and balance sheet should all tie into one another and into the supplemental schedules.

Many, possibly most of the financial forecasts I have seen start with a top down approach. By this I mean they forecast revenue by assuming they will obtain a certain percent of the market share in the third or fifth year. It goes something like this, "This is a $10 billion dollar industry and if we can just get 1% market share we will have a $100 million in revenue by year five."

Sophisticated early stage investors hate this type of forecasting. It shows the business has put little or no thought into their sales and marketing strategy and I guarantee you they will either turn you down out of hand or completely rework your forecasts. Outside of commodity businesses, how many businesses have you heard of that have one percent market penetration? They either have at least 5% or they are eaten alive by those that have 35% or 70% market penetration.

The way to forecast revenue is one sale at a time, then ten, then one hundred, then one thousand. You have this great product. Who needs it the most? Can they afford it? If so that is your first prospect. Who are the next ten? Go after them. Once sold who's next. This way you have a step by step sales strategy. If the first ten are in the same region, that's your first regional office. If they are scattered all over the world, maybe you need to start by utilizing, manufacturer representatives. So many more questions get answered when you use a bottom up approach to sales forecasts!

Preparing quality financial projections for a new or early stage company is difficult and time consuming but it is the only way an investor or the founder can be confident that the business can succeed financially. Someone experienced in preparing quality forecasts should be intimately involved in this process.

A three to five minute presentation, referred to by many as an "elevator pitch" is important for anyone selling anything including an investment in ones business. Here is why. You never know when you might have a chance encounter with someone who may want to invest in your business. You may only have three to five minutes with this person and need to have an organized sales pitch for that length of time. The term elevator pitch comes from the amount of time you might have in an elevator with someone but there are many other occasions where your time is limited with someone - at a cocktail party; waiting in line for tickets, to pay for groceries or at the airport; or during a break at a business conference.

The pitch must identify the problem being addressed and the size of the market, explain your solution and why it is better than others, briefly describe the management team and why they can execute on the plan and explain how much it will cost. Most importantly you must identify yourself and your company and leave behind contact information, hopefully in the form of a business card. You do not have time to go into detail on any of the points just mentioned. The purpose of the elevator pitch is to pique someone's interest so that they may follow up.

"Investor Pitch" Pointers

☐ Tips on presenting to potential investors
- Brevity
- Identify the Pain
- What is the size of the market?
- What differentiates your product from possible competitors?
- Describe your route to market
- Show off your team
- Summary of Financial Projections and when you reach breakeven
- Don't Forget the ask!!! How much Money are you looking for?

Figure 7 – Investor Pitch Pointers.

An entrepreneur seeking funds should also have a 15-20 minute power point or similar presentation prepared before seeking investors. This is another item that you may not need at the outset but you never know how quickly the process will advance to this stage and you need to be prepared.

A quality presentation of this length takes time to prepare. There may be data that needs to collected and graphics that need to be generated. The entire presentation needs to be consistent with what is stated in the business plan and the figures that are in the financial projections. All of this takes longer than most anticipate and then you need sufficient time to practice, practice and practice. You need to be prepared for whatever questions arise during or after your presentation. As part of your practice sessions, have a business advisor or another small business owner ask questions to see if you're prepared.

What's not in the Investor Presentation

"If you find yourself deep in the hole...stop digging."
Will Rogers

□ Technical details

□ Voluminous Attachments, e.g. Testimonials, Patent Application, Letters of Interest

□ Use of the term, "Conservative Projections!!!" Company prepared projections are seldom conservative and the term is a red flag to Investors

□ Too many slides– Power Point is the most abused substitute for good speaking. Limit to a few strong visuals

Figure 8 – What's not in the Investor Presentation.

You are now ready to submit your proposal to an angel investor, network or fund. What happens from here? Usually, the proposal to an early stage investor consists of either a business plan or perhaps only the executive summary to the plan. As mentioned earlier, the process for a venture capital firm will normally be more formalized than a single angel investor, so Let's look at the venture capitalist's typical process and note differences between them and angel networks or angel funds when they arise.

One other point worth mentioning is that a business' chances of getting past the initial review increases dramatically if the proposal is referred into the investor by someone they know and trust. Proposals that come in cold are referred to as "over the transom" and are many times given only a cursory look. Some times business advisors, coaches or business associates know angels or venture capitalists and can get you an audience. In an angel or venture fund it is great if they can get your proposal in front of an associate they know. It's even better if they know a partner in the firm.

If you do not know any investors another way to get known is through angel and investor forums. These forums differ in the length of time you have to present and in the selection process but they are a way to get in front of an audience, practice your pitch and network with investors. After an investor sees that you have a credible business and can make a quality presentation you have a much greater chance of getting a second look.

The presentations at these events can be as short as three minute elevator pitch or as long as fifteen to thirty minute investor presentation. Some of the larger events actually have investors evaluate the applicants to pick the best fifteen to thirty deals. If you are selected, find out who the evaluators were and contact them. They like your deal well enough to select you for a presentation. Finally, many times these events will let you practice in front of a group of coaches that will provide suggestions to improve your presentation prior to the event. Even if you do not get any leads from the forum it provides you with input and experience you cannot get elsewhere.

I should mention here to expect that the entire investment process from initial review to legal closing to take 90 days or more. There are many factors that determine whether this period can be cut to 80 days or will last 120 days, not the least of which is the responsiveness of the entrepreneur to requests for clarification or additional material.

6.

INVESTOR'S REVIEW AND ANALYSIS OF A BUSINESS PROPOSAL

When an investor gets your proposal the first thing they will do is a review to see if it makes sense and fits their investment criteria. All investors have investment criteria whether they are informal as may be the case of some individual angel investors or quite formal like a large VC firm.

If the proposal makes sense does it fit with what I, the investor is seeking? Figure 9 summarizes what is looked at in this initial review.

After the initial review the investor will decide whether to move forward to the next stage in the process. If the decision is to move forward the VC or angel may contact the entrepreneur for more information or they may just ask for a meeting, either at their offices or the entrepreneur's business. This meeting may be just to delve further into the business and get questions asked or it may be to have the entrepreneur make a formal presentation, probably to one or two of the firm's staff. This is where the 15-20 minute presentation mentioned earlier comes into play.

Equity Investor's Initial Review

- ☐ Is it the right size?
- ☐ Is it the in our territory?
- ☐ Does the business proposition make sense?
- ☐ Is it at the right stage?
- ☐ Will it grow fast enough?
- ☐ Is management adequate?
- ☐ Does the product/service work?
- ☐ Are there adequate barriers to entry
- ☐ Is it reasonable?

Figure 9 – Equity Investor's Initial Review.

For a month possibly even more there will be requests for additional material, discussions about the assumptions in the financial forecasts and clarification of data submitted. The VC staff will do there own market analysis, assessment of management, sales and marketing, accounting and operations.

There may be several more meetings between venture staff and the business involved during this time. In the case of an individual angel investor it is likely most of these interactions will be with the angel him or her self, but in the case of the venture firm the entrepreneur will most likely be dealing with an associate during this period and not a partner. This of course differs depending on how a firm operates and to some extent the size of the firm. Some times a partner will get involved immediately following the initial review. It is also more likely that a partner gets involved early if they have a particular interest in a given proposal. A good example of this is when a proposal has been referred in by someone that partner knows well and trusts, possibly someone they have co-invested with in the past or the CEO of a former successful portfolio company.

At any point in the process the investor may decide not to make an investment. After the initial review if they wish to continue forward a meeting may be scheduled where the management team of the prospective company is asked to make a presentation to one, some or all of the firm's partners. This meeting may be scheduled for as long as an hour or even more but the formal presentation shouldn't be longer than thirty minutes. There will be questions and the partners may come in late and not stay for the entire time. It's not that they are rude, although this might be the case with a few I've known, it's just that they are extremely busy and are being pulled in several directions at once.

This is why this presentation, and actually all investment presentations, should make all the salient points early in the presentation and fill in the details towards the end. Generally, a formal meeting with partners will not occur unless the staff is seriously considering recommending that a term sheet be issued to the business.

If all goes well at this presentation the staff will get back to the business with any follow-up questions and then probably perform some sort of formal rating or grading exercise. I have used different templates for this depending on the situation. Appendix A, "Business Opportunity Grade" covers the major factors that a VC or angel will evaluate at this stage.

This process will differ slightly when an angel network or angel fund is involved. It will begin the same with the cursory review of the business plan to determine whether or not the business meets the minimum criteria of the group or angel fund. With some angel networks a copy of the executive summary is distributed to each angel in the network to solicit their possible interest. If it is determined that the proposal meets the group's or fund's criteria, a meeting of some or all of the angels in the group will be held, where they will hear a 15-20 minute presentation from the business.

If an angel network, the group will decide whether enough people are interested in the investment to move forward. If so, one or more of the angels will be assigned to further analyze the business and investment opportunity and report back to the group. If after further review it is recommended that a term sheet be issued the group would be polled to decide how many in the group would like to participate in the investment and at what dollar level.

An angel fund with professional management would move forward, at this point similar to a venture fund. An angel fund without professional management might assign individual angels to look into the proposal further, much like an angel network. In either case if it is decided to move to a term sheet, the fund would be the investor and not the individual angels.

7.

VALUATION, RECOMMENDATION, TERM SHEET AND CLOSING

At this point the staff is fairly comfortable that the product is viable, the market is large enough, the sales and marketing strategy makes sense and the management team is capable of taking the company to the next level. It is now time to put the details of a proposed investment together.

Valuation

Some time before a term sheet is prepared a valuation of the business will be performed by the angel or venture capital firm to determine what percentage of the business the investor will receive for its investment. The investor will base this valuation on financial projections, usually using the forecast that the company provided as a starting point. They will review assumptions and revise the forecasts where they feel it is necessary. They may even create their own financial model if it is felt the originals are based on shaky assumptions. Almost always revenue forecasts, gross margins, profit margins and cash flow will be discounted.

Once the forecasts are revised the investor must decide the rate of return desired in order for the investment to make sense to the investor. Most investors have a range in which all investments must fall. In many cases this range may be quite wide, for example 35% to 50%. In this example, if risk is considered to be relatively low compared to Other investments the firm makes, the required rate will be closer to 35%. If it is relatively high it will be closer to 50%. Risk will be determined based on the market, management team, the margins, barriers to entry and many other factors.

The investor will then calculate a value usually based on some multiple of EbITDA (earnings before interest, taxes, depreciation and amortization) in the third, fourth or fifth year of the investment. Depending on the industry a multiple of revenue or some other financial measure may be used. The investor will then use a valuation model to calculate the percentage ownership it must have to get the desired return.

There are a number of valuation models one can find in the college finance text books that may be used as a basis for the valuation. Early stage investors may use one of these as the basis for its model but will almost certainly adjust it to fit their own needs. Even if an investor uses a particular valuation model do not expect them to reveal which one it is.

On several occasions I have had entrepreneurs attempt to argue the value based on one accepted model or another. One will find that valuation at the early stages is as much an art as it is a science and that almost any valuation can be rationalized depending on the assumptions made. The fact is the investor has the money and they will decide the valuation. This not to say that they will not leave some room in the valuation for negotiations, most of the time they will.

Recommendation

I have mentioned moving to a term sheet a couple of times in the preceding paragraphs but there is an important step before we get there. Actually, a draft of the term sheet will probably be prepared soon after The valuation is complete but a recommendation to the venture firm's investment committee must be made and voted on before the entrepreneur or business ever gets to see the terms sheet.

Fund staff will prepare this recommendation that could be ten to twenty pages in length that analyzes each major function of the business – management, operations, financial and accounting, marketing and sales and etc. The recommendation will generally include a proposed term sheet in anticipation of making an investment. The staff working on this recommendation could be a team that includes a partner and associate(s), just a partner or just associates. In my experience, at this point there is generally a partner who has been involved with the valuation, term sheet and recommendation at some level. If the deal gets to the investment committee this person will act as a champion for the deal with the other partners.

The staff recommendation will be presented to the investment committee of the fund, which is made up of some or all of the partners. The committee will discuss the recommendation at length and vote whether or not to move forward with an investment. In this meeting the committee may elect to change the proposed terms in one way or another. Decisions of investment committees usually require a super majority of the committee (or of those present) to move forward. My experience is that this could be a two-thirds, three-fourths or unanimous affirmative vote. The last fund I was involved with it took a unanimous vote of those present at the meeting.

The Term Sheet

So now we are at the point of a term sheet where all the terms of an investment if made are delineated. Early in the first chapter I said, *"While the details of an angel or venture capital deal can get quite complicated the basic concept is quite simple."* The term sheet is where it gets quite complicated. Below is a simple definition of a term sheet but the devil is in the details.

Term Sheet – A document that summarizes the details of an investment proposal usually by a venture capital firm that is used to prepare final investment agreements.

Term sheets are usually in the form of a letter to the prospective portfolio company. It can be two to three pages long and spell out the general terms of an investment such as share price, type of security and the pre money valuation of the company or it can be six to ten pages long and go into much more detail concerning covenants, conditions precedent and pre-emptive rights. A sample term sheet can be found in Appendix B.

My experience, mostly in the Midwestern United States has been with the longer form of the term sheet. I prefer the longer form because that way most features of the investment are spelled out up front leaving fewer surprises when documents are reviewed or at the closing.

The term sheet is one of the most important documents in the investment process but possibly the most confusing and misunderstood. It can be disheartening when you think you have convinced someone to invest in your company at a reasonable valuation, only to find out there are pages of conditions that take away control, dilute ownership and require more work on your part. Many entrepreneurs have a value they feel they must get. They are so fixed on value that they value.

The first part of the term sheet letter looks like a pleased to inform the entrepreneur that they are considering an investment in the entrepreneur's company. It goes on to say that below you will find the general terms of the proposed investment. There may be a few sentences on such things as non-disclosure, exclusivity and confidentiality.

Usually, the final paragraph of the traditional letter part of the term sheet will explain that thus far the investor is relying on the information supplied by the company and has done little or no due diligence. The final sentence of this paragraph says something like, "Our proposal remains subject to, among other things: (i) completion of business, accounting, and legal due diligence to the satisfaction of Investor; (ii) the negotiation and completion of satisfactory legal documentation relating to our investment, and; (iii) the formal approval of Investor's Investment Committee. It may also say something to the effect that if any significant negative changes in the company's performance or financial condition occurs between the date of this letter and the closing that the investor in its sole discretion can withdraw its proposal. This part of the letter really gives the investor an escape if they decide they really don't want to make the investment after all.

The letter then goes into all of the terms of the investment in sort of an outline format. The first part of this outline section usually explains the form of investment. In other words, how much the investor is willing to finance, what class of stock it will receive, how many shares of stock and what percentage ownership the investor will receive, and what if any dividend will be distributed.

One of the most important concepts to understand when reviewing and negotiating a term sheet is "stated value" vs. "real value". In the financial industry the value stated on a term sheet as the pre-money valuation or post money valuation is referred to as the "stated value." This is rarely the "real value" or the value after all factors are considered. What often occurs is that the entrepreneur does not fully understand the difference. He or she has a value in mind and since the price per share in the term sheet reflects that value they accept it on its face, even though they may be uncomfortable with all the term sheet's conditions.

This "form of the investment" section of the term sheet really defines the "stated" value of the business and begins to Define the "real" value . This is explained in more detail in the sidebar entitled, "The 'Real Value of Your Business."

After the form of investment is outlined, the term sheet goes on to explain a number of "investor rights." or covenants. Here is a description some of the most common:

Stock Redemption

This allows the new investor to redeem its stock beginning on some date in the future. The redemption price is usually the purchase price plus any accrued dividends that have not been paid. There may be an additional interest rate included, as well.

Conversion

Allows the new investor to convert its preferred stock into common stock at any time, usually on a one-for-one basis. It also usually states that the preferred stock will automatically be converted into common stock upon the closing of a qualified Initial Public Offering or a sale of the company's stock at a certain price or multiple.

The "Real Value" of Your Business

Many angel or venture capitalist have proposed the terms of investments dozens of times before and know how to play on the emotions of the entrepreneur. They can often give the entrepreneur the "stated value" they seek and still obtain the "real value" they desire. There are a number of provisions in the typical term sheet that significantly alter the value stated as a per share price. Some may reduce the real value by 50% or more!

Let's take a look at provisions found in most term sheets. First of all the institutional investor will most likely ask for "participating preferred shares." This is a far cry from the common shares the founders and their family and friends own. The "preferred" means that if the company is sold or wound up in any other way, say liquidation or bankruptcy, the preferred shareholder gets its money out before any common shareholder receives a payout.

The "participating" means that after the preferred shareholders receive their original amount back, they split the remainder on a pro rata ownership basis with the common shareholders. To make this even more dilutive to the common shareholders, the amount the preferred shareholders receive before any other money is distributed is many times a multiple of their original investment. For instance, it is not uncommon For the "liquidation preference" to be 150%-200% of the original investment During recessionary periods there have been instances of it being even higher!

Another feature of Participating preferred stock is that it typically carries a dividend. The dividend rate is dependent upon the current credit market but it is not unusual for it to be 7%-8% annually. Usually in venture deals the dividend is deferred until the company is sold, merged, wound up or goes public but must be paid prior to any money going to common shareholders. If you add this to the liquidation preference, the investor could be receiving two to three times their investment back before the common shareholders share the remainder with them. This is no big deal if the company goes public for 10-20 times the original value but if it is just modestly successful it can leave the common shareholders with little or nothing!

In some deals there may also be warrants issued to the investor either for doing certain things for the company or if the company does not meet certain conditions. These warrants may be converted to stock well below the market value of the stock lowering the value of the common stock even more.

The easiest way to explain the difference between stated value and real value is to provide an example. Let's keep it simple and say that there are no warrants involved.

ABC Ventures invests $1 million in Willy's Widgets for 20% of the company's stock. This means that the stated pre-money valuation of Willy's Widgets is $4 million. Another way to say This is that the value of the stock owned by investors prior to the new investment is $4 million. The stated post-money valuation or the value after the new investment is in will be $5 million.

Let's assume that ABC Ventures stock has a 1.5 times liquidation preference with an 8% cumulative annual dividend. Five years from the time of the investment a buyer proposes to buy the company for $10 million. If the stated value was the same as the real value, ABC Ventures would double its money and receive $2 million and the other investors shares would double in value and they would receive $8 million as a group.

Now let's look at the real value. Because ABC's stock is preferred they get their principal out first and since the liquidation value is 1.5 times the principal they receive $1.5 million before anyone else receives anything - but wait. They had an 8% annual dividend that was cumulative over the five year period so they receive 8% x 5years = 40%. Forty percent of $1 million is $400,000 plus the $1.5 million preference means that ABC gets $1.9 million before any of the proceeds are divided pro rata.

This leaves a balance of $8.1 million to be divided 20% to ABC and 80% to the remaining shareholders. This means that ABC receives another $1.6 million and the remaining shareholders receive $6.5 million. Once the $1.6 million is added to the 1.9 million, ABC receives a total of $3.5 million or 35% of the total value, not 20%! Of course, what the "real" value turns out to be, depends greatly on what price the shares of the company are ultimately sold.

So what is the real value? The real pre-money value, or the value of the current shareholders stock is not $4 million but instead $1.86 million! Quite a significant difference and we haven't discussed other provisions that could lower the real value further if certain contingencies occur. Here are the most common of those.

There are usually anti-dilution provisions, likely in the form of "ratchets," which require the company issue additional shares, in the event that stock is subsequently sold at a lower price, say in a subsequent round of financing than the price paid by the original institutional investor. A "full ratchet" basis requires enough stock be issued to bring the value up to that of the new investor. A weighted ratchet basis makes up some of the value lost but not all of it. In either case the "real" pre-money value of the original investment drops even further.

There are other provisions that might directly or indirectly affect value. The two not mentioned in this example for simplicity reasons that are most common and have a significant impact on the value are "ratchets" and warrants. There is more discussion of both of these mechanisms in the body of this chapter.

I am not providing this example to paint the investor as some sort of charlatan, after all I was active in the venture capital industry for twenty years. These are ways for the investor to protect their downside and many times used to come to agreement on a difference in valuation. An angel or VC might even pose the terms to the entrepreneur something like this: "We are not confident that you can meet your projections and if you do not, the value of the company will certainly be lower but we are willing to accept your valuation if you will allow us to protect ourselves from under performance. If in fact, you truly believe in your valuation you shouldn't mind these provisions. They will not affect your return significantly if you perform at the level indicated."

What I do wish to communicate is that the entrepreneur, his or her advisors and the other shareholders need to review the investment proposal or term sheet with eyes wide open. Too often the entrepreneur does not understand the impact of the provisions or is too optimistic about company performance and then a year or so after the investment is made when things do not go as planned feels like he or she has been mislead or worse cheated. No one, including the new investor wants a contentious relationship once in the deal. It's better to negotiate the terms as an informed participant. In this way you can either decide it is the best deal you are likely to get and accept it or decide to turn the offer down and look somewhere else.

Liquidation Preference

In the event of any liquidation, dissolution or winding up of the Company, the new investor is entitled to receive, an amount equal to a certain multiple of the Purchase Price plus any accrued but unpaid dividends. This multiple is usually between one times and two times the purchase price. After this is paid any remaining funds and assets of the Company are usually distributed pro rata among the new investors and other shareholders.

Anti-Dilution Preference

Term sheet provision that is designed to protect the outside investor from the possibility of a lower valuation in subsequent rounds of financing. The most common method of protecting against anti-dilution is a ratchet.

A "ratchet"

Is a mechanism that provides the investor additional shares of stock either for free or at a reduced price. There are "full ratchets" and "weighted ratchets." With a "full ratchet" the investor receives additional shares for free so that the average cost per share is the same as the new investor. With a "weighted ratchet" the investor has the ability to acquire additional shares such that the cost per share is the same as the weighted average price of subsequently issued shares.

Voting Rights

Allows the preferred shareholder to vote its share as if they held common stock equal to the number of shares they would receive if converted. It also allows the preferred shareholders to vote separately from the common shareholders on specific issues.

Protective Provisions

Requires the company to obtain approval from the new investors prior to taking action on activities that may directly affect the value of the new investor's preferred stock, such as:

- Repurchase or redemption of any shares;
- Alter or change the rights, preferences or privileges of the new investor's stock, including any amendments to the Articles of Incorporation affecting the rights and privileges of the new investor;
- Authorize or issue shares of any class of stock having preference or priority as to dividends or assets superior to, or on parity with the new investor;
- Increase the authorized number of shares of preferred stock;
- Increase the number of Company Directors;
- Any sale, merger or consolidation of the Company;

- The liquidation or dissolution of the Company; or,
- The declaration or payment of a dividend on the stock.

Preemptive Rights

Gives the new investor the right to purchase up to its pro rata Share of any offering of stock by the Company at the same price and terms as the Company offers to other potential investors.

Right of First Refusal

Gives the new investor the right to purchase any Common or Preferred shares offered for sale by other shareholders of the Company on the same price and terms as they are offered to third parties, prior to them being sold to an outside party.

Co-Sale Agreement

Gives the new investor the right to participate on a *pari passu* basis with any other shareholder in sales of common or preferred shares to third parties.

Registration Rights

Gives the new investor certain rights to have its stock registered in the event that the business in which it is investing goes public. This allows the investor to sell its stock in the public market.

Exclusivity

This gives the new investor an exclusive right to invest at the terms and in the amount stated in the term sheet for some specified period of time, usually a few months.

Purchase of Warrants

The purchase of warrants is more often found in later stage deals but is sometimes found in early stage deals, as well. It is a security, with an attached derivative giving the holder the right to purchase shares of the underlying security at a specified price at some specified future date. One way to think of a warrant is to think of it as being similar to a stock option.

Following the covenants or "investor rights" in a term sheet is the "Conditions Precedent" section. Conditions precedent sometimes referred to as "Conditions to Closing" are items that must be fulfilled prior to the investment documents being executed and the funds disbursed. Some of these conditions can be found in almost any term sheets. Others are specific to a certain deal. It may be something that the investor knows is missing or needs to be addressed but does not wish to hold up the term sheet until it is resolved.

Below are a few common conditions precedent:

- Completion of due diligence investigation satisfactory to the investor in its sole discretion;
- No material adverse change in the business' operations, financial condition or prospects;
- No litigation threatened or commenced that might challenge the transaction
- No material increase in liabilities or material increase in assets of the business;
- The company's board and shareholders have taken all action necessary to affect the transaction.

As in a loan that you may receive for your business or a mortgage to buy a new house, the legal and closing costs of the investment transaction will be the responsibility of the business. This will be stated somewhere in the term sheet and the costs can be quite substantial. My suggestion is to try to negotiate a cap on these expenses. I have seen this done in a number of cases. In this way you will know the net proceeds of the investment upfront.

The closing paragraph of the term sheet will point out that the term sheet is not meant to be binding on either party's part and might look something like this:

Please understand that this letter is not to be considered a commitment by (the new investor) but rather is our statement of interest to effect the proposed transaction in accordance with terms and subject to conditions outlined above. Except for the last sentence of this paragraph, this letter should not be construed as a binding agreement on the part of any of the parties. If the terms as outlined herein are satisfactory, please acknowledge the acceptance of such by signing the acknowledgement below and returning this signed letter to our offices no later than _____ p.m. CDT, _____(day of the week),_____(date) . By signing below, you agree to treat this letter and its contents as being highly confidential and agree not to disclose any of its contents to any persons other than the companies' officers, directors and previously identified advisors.

I know this discussion of the term sheet was quite lengthy and it might leave one feeling like the task of reviewing and negotiating a term sheet is daunting. If it has left that impression then I have accomplished what I intended. It is extremely difficult to truly understand the impact that the terms of an early stage investment agreement can have on the value of a company, how it operates and whether or not it succeeds. In my mind this may be the most critical phase of the investment process and yet is likely to be completed in a week to ten days.

There are some things you should know going into the term sheet negotiation. First of all when you sign a term sheet you are giving the investor an exclusive right to invest in the business. There are some investors that will use this to re-negotiate the terms especially if they can show that the business' financial circumstances have changed. They know you cannot go any where else until the period is over. Even if you somehow get out of the exclusivity clause other VCs will be hesitant to deal with someone that did not honor the previous exclusivity clause. Make sure you know who you are dealing with. Try to find out before signing a term sheet whether the investor you are dealing with has a habit trying to re-negotiate.

Try to get a term sheet from more than one investor before signing any term sheet. Most VCs and angels have big egos. They don't like to lose out to a peer. Get them bidding on the terms of the deal and you have the upper hand instead of them.

Early stage investors, especially fund managers are quite adept at negotiating a term sheet. Most of them have been involved in dozens of negotiations. There will be things they will negotiate away quite easily and there other things they must have. They know what the financial impact of say lowering the number of shares they receive in exchange for a higher liquidation preference. They may even stick things in the term sheet they don't really want in order to make you feel like you won when they give it back to you.

If you and the investor just cannot come to an agreement on the valuation you may wish to suggest some sort of performance based valuation. Perhaps the entrepreneur gets a higher valuation but agrees to allow the investor additional warrants if projections are not met after the first or second year. The opposite scenario is for the investor to get its valuation but allow the business to "earn back" shares based on meeting or exceeding projections. I am not suggesting this sort of arrangement is always palatable but it has been done in instances where valuation cannot be agreed upon.

Finally, try to understand how badly the investor wishes to do your deal. There are deals that the investor salivates over. They will jump hoops to get the deal done. There are others that they may say, "This isn't the greatest deal in the world but if we can get the terms we ask for it's worth doing." If you negotiate fiercely on the first you may get what you want but if you do the same on the second deal you may not even get a response. You need to try to assess where you stand.

It is always a good idea to have a professional that is experienced in valuations and term sheet evaluation look over the offer to help you understand what it means and how much the company needs to be worth at the time of exit in order for you to get a satisfactory return. Finally, an attorney experienced in securities law should always review the legal aspects of the term sheet or offer before you sign. Venture capitalists and their attorneys deal with term sheets routinely and you need to be represented by someone who has dealt with investments of this kind, as well!

It is ok to turn down a term sheet that just doesn't work for you. After all, there are some unscrupulous investors out there and some that just don't know what they are doing. But if you find you have turned down two or three and they all have similar terms, maybe it's you. Too many entrepreneurs, probably most of them have an inflated idea of the value of their business or technology. Remember only a very small percentage of early stage equity deals get done and if you have turned down a couple already you may not get another chance.

I was the lead partner on a deal about six years ago that had three different venture capital funds submit term sheets to them. I had co-invested with the other two in the past and knew that at least one of them had a lower valuation than I did. We revised our terms twice and went back to the company trying to get the deal. Finally, we walked away. Several years later I was talking to their advisor and happened to ask her what ever happened to that deal. She explained that the company was still around growing slowly each year. She confided in me that we were the best deal and she advised them to take our deal – They weren't going to get anything better. In the end no one did the deal and they never had another opportunity to raise equity capital.

Due Diligence

Once the term sheet is accepted the investor will begin its detailed due diligence process. In all likelihood, some due diligence was conducted prior to issuing the term sheet but the investor does not want to go to the expense and time to do much of this tedious process without knowing whether or not the entrepreneur will accept the terms.

Many people confuse the initial review and analysis of the business itself with due diligence but there is a distinct difference. Throughout this guide I have usually provided definitions in my own words, but the definition of due diligence found in an article by Harvey and Lusch is simple and yet captures the essence of the term. It is, "The process of assembling and verifying the information related to an investment decision, whether on behalf of others or oneself." [1]

So what information is assembled and verified? Some of it is similar to what a bank might look at when deciding whether or not to provide a loan to an individual or business, other pieces are quite different. Appendix C includes items that I have looked at when conducting due diligence. Each case is a bit different depending upon the investor's intuition, the industry and management Background. Some items in the list will not apply to some deals while other items may be added in certain circumstances. This list is not meant to be exhaustive but instead is provided to give the entrepreneur an indication of what is in store for them.

The more items that are assembled in one place or that are readily available to the investor the quicker the process flows. If material is missing or board minutes, resolutions and other records have not been kept the due diligence process can get quite protracted and in rare instances can even mean the deal never gets to a closing.

Once due diligence is completed many venture firms will take the deal back to the partners for a final blessing. Those working on the deal may review the final terms of the deal and the findings of due diligence. This gives the partners one more

[1] Harvey, Michael G. and Robert F. Lusch, "Expanding the Nature and Scope of Due Diligence." *Journal of Business Venturing,* 10 (January 1995): 1-22.

chance to make sure the terms are as they anticipated and that all the "T's" are crossed and "I's" are dotted.

Legal and Closing

The final phase of the investment process is drafting of legal documents and then closing on the investment. Legal costs can skyrocket if the attorneys for the investor and the company's attorney decide to squabble over language in the documents. Each time new language is drafted the bill goes up and the time to closing gets extended. Try to get the two sides to agree on all language between the first and second drafts of the agreements, instead of requiring that four or five drafts be prepared.

Some of the legal documents typical in an equity investment include; a Shareholder Agreement, Stock Purchase Agreement, Investment Agreement, Employment and Noncompetition Agreements, Registration Agreement, Revised Articles of Incorporation and By-Laws and Attorneys' Opinions. Depending on the deal there may be other documents, as well.

8.

Working With A New Investor

As you probably realize by now, the angel or venture capital investor does not just write you a check and leave you alone until its time to cash in. You should expect that the investor will be active rather than passive. They will almost always have a seat on the board and may have the right to have a second person attend board meetings as an observer. They may even have two seats on the board. Their involvement does not end there.

The earlier stage the company, the more involvement there will likely be. Some seed stage investors call portfolio companies several times a week and if things are not going well they will be in contact daily. In seed and start-up companies they may even have a member of the VC firm's staff as an interim officer in the company. For early stage companies expect that the investor will require monthly board meetings, expansion stage and later may only require quarterly meetings. Regardless of the stage of the company, monthly financial statements and sales reports will be required to be submitted.

There may be other planning and reporting that is required that the company may or may not be accustomed. Many firms want a strategic plan developed and possibly a staffing plan, before the investment is made. They may have the company develop a 90-100 day action plan for the period immediately post-investment. This is a critical time in the company's life because they have a large sum of money to put to work and it needs to be done quickly and effectively. Certainly, the investor will require an annual budget be developed. If the business is on a calendar year for accounting purposes this process will probably begin in the summer or early autumn.

Good news can wait. Bad news is best delivered early.

After money has gone into a portfolio business, investors see themselves as advisors as much as anything. They expect to speak with the entrepreneur between board meetings and monthly reports and they expect the entrepreneur to inform them of any significant developments, good or bad. The only way they can help the business optimize the opportunity when a good development takes place is to provide advice early in the process. More importantly the only way to minimize damage is to find out about it as soon after it happens as possible.

Communication is key. All seasoned early stage investors know that things are going to go wrong from time to time. What they cannot tolerate is not hearing about it for days or even weeks after it occurs. The longer one waits to take action the more the problem is compounded. More than once, as an investor I was kept in the dark too long to be able to provide an acceptable solution. Some of these businesses went broke because of this lack of communication!

Some investors unfortunately are not very good advisors, but most that have significant experience are well worth the time it takes to ask questions. They should help with management recruitment, hiring decisions, compensation issues, marketing, operations and a myriad of other issues. They generally have a hefty "rolodex" that will help find professional services, suppliers, strategic partners, managers and even customers. Listen to their advice and in most cases it's probably best to follow it. Remember, however that in the end management is ultimately responsible for the success of the business. You do not need to always heed the investors advice, especially if your certain it will lead to disaster or if it just doesn't seem ethical or proper.

When things go wrong expect the investor to become more involved. They are doing this to protect their investment. If things are bad enough they may put a person in the company to help manage the business out of trouble and to see if changes in systems, staffing and even top management need to be made. If a company is at risk of failure expect that a venture capitalist will bring in a turn around specialist, either one on staff or a contracted specialist that the VC has had experience with in the past. When things get to this point, the entrepreneur should realize that the investor has moved from helping the business maximize value to making sure his or her investment is protected.

Different investors will be more or less involved than others and what I have suggested their involvement will be is only an example of what might occur. Expect that they will be more involved than you expected. Investors will generally work with you if you work with them. They will not hesitate, however to bring in new management or make other changes if the current management is not acceptable. Most have learned from experience that people generally wait too long to make difficult decisions.

So after learning about what angel and venture capital investing is, seeing if your business can attract it and what the process is to obtain equity financing there is only one critical question remaining. Is angel or venture capital financing right for you and your business? It certainly has its upside but an entrepreneur needs to decide whether it fits with what he or she wishes to accomplish, whether it fits his or her lifestyle and personality. In the final chapter we will take a look at both the pluses and minuses of angel and venture funding.

9.

Is Angel Of Venture Capital The Right Fit For You Or Your Business?

There is nothing wrong with deciding that angel or venture capital is wrong for you or your business. Certainly it allows companies to penetrate, even saturate markets; grow rapidly and even go public if the market is right. Here are some reasons people decide that it is not right for them.

First of all raising angel or venture capital is time consuming and takes away from operating your business. More often than not, businesses suffer during the months it takes to raise capital. From the time you decide to raise equity capital to actually obtaining cash can take anywhere from six months to a year or more. It takes staff away from normal duties to revise business plans, prepare slide presentations and develop financial projections. It takes the management away from the business, contacting prospective investors, making presentations, answering questions and working with accountants and attorneys.

Secondly once outside equity is invested in a business the entrepreneur and management team lose some degree of freedom to operate as they wish. Once outside equity is invested the entrepreneur, management, family and friends are not the only owners. There is an active board of directors and there are milestones that must be met, approvals that must be obtained, covenants that must be honored and reports that must be prepared. The investor will expect you to work 60 or more hours a week and the rest of the management along with you. There will be disagreements between management and investors and there will be pressure to perform.

Do you wish to maximize company value quickly and then sell the company or go public? Because once the outside investor is in the deal maximizing value and exiting the deal in three to seven years is paramount. If your dream is to leave your business to your son, daughter or loyal employee then angel or venture capital are not for you. But if you are the type that likes to start things and then move on to another challenge it might be perfect.

Do you wish to grow rapidly? This question is similar to the last one but there is some difference. If you are the type that wants to make sure the product you developed is perfect before going to market or if you need to have a personal relationship with each of your customers, growing rapidly will probably not work. If you cannot delegate and want to be involved in every decision your business makes then the business will not maximize sales and thus will probably not grow fast enough to satisfy investors.

Are you willing to bring in additional management, probably even someone that will be your superior? Data shows that the majority of founders whose businesses receive venture capital do not retain the top management position and many are no longer active in management after a year or two into the investment. Many of the other top management in the business will likely be replaced during the time a venture capitalist has an investment in a business.

Its not that it is intended, instead it is that the job either gets to be too much for the person's talent or personality or that management disagrees with the direction that the new investors wish to take the company.

Can you and the investor agree on the Business Model? If not, it is better to walk away from a deal. All too often I have seen situations where the investor and management do not agree how to sell the product, which channels to use or whether or not to outsource manufacturing. The entrepreneur desperate to receive financing capitulates maybe thinking they can change the investors mind once the deal is done. It usually does not work this way, the business suffers from lack of direction and someone loses their job, usually not the investor.

Changing ones lifestyle is a big part of whether or not you take outside investment. The investor may be reasonable about certain things but remember many of these people became wealthy because they were workaholics. If you're the type that wants to be able to turn the cell phone off at 9:00 pm and not turn it off until 7:00 the following morning this may not be for you.

Some investors will honor your free time when at all possible but others will call at night on weekends and while you are on vacation, whether or not it is an emergency. If you're the type that wants to take off early to get a golf game or go fishing with buddies then it may be best to find an alternative means of financing your business. These investors have serious money in the game and they want you to work at least as hard as they do or once did.

All of this sounds pretty rough, but maybe it should. After all someone is probably putting millions of dollars in a business that probably statistically only has about a 20% chance of surviving! On the other hand, there are plenty of people who have the personalities not only to survive in this type of environment but thrive.

Many entrepreneurs are already working 60 hours or more a week, rarely see their families and will Do almost anything to see their passion succeed. They see the opportunity to become wealthy right along with the investor and have the confidence in themselves to make it happen. They get bored easily and need another opportunity in three to five years. They can adapt to an ever changing environment and do not lose sleep over losing their' but other people's money.

If you have the personality, drive and lifestyle mentioned above then you may wish to pursue an angel or venture investment in your business. Even if you are missing some of the traits you may wish to swallow hard and investigate the possibility further. In some cases it is the only way for a business to survive.

If you decide to pursue an angel or venture capital investor you need to do your due diligence while they're doing theirs. In meetings you have had with them do they feel like someone you will be able to work with or does it seem like they are full of hot air? Are they personable; are they respectful of you, your knowledge and experience?

Ask them for the contacts at businesses where they have made investments. Call them and speak to them about negotiating the terms of an investment, how the investor is to work with on an ongoing basis and how they react in times of crisis. Ask the investor what there experience has been with companies like yours. If biographies of the investors or partners are not readily available on their website or in promotional literature ask them for a bio or resume. Find out what their success rate has been in past investments.

Just as the investor needs to find the right fit the business does, as well. There are VCs that I would not co-invest with when I was in the business and there are ones that you should not take on as investors. They will be a part of your business for three to seven years!

CONCLUSION

There is so much more to fully understanding "early" stage equity investing than what is covered in this guide, but what I have chosen to leave out takes either education or experience in finance and investing that is not common among those starting a new business.

What I hope has been communicated is that early stage equity financing is not for all small businesses, in fact it is for relatively few. Just because a business may not qualify for equity financing does not mean that the business cannot be highly successful. Thirdly, even if a business qualifies for equity financing it may not be right for the business or the owner(s). I hope I have provided a flavor for what types of businesses might have a chance at angel or venture funding and why. If this is all that is accomplished, the guide has been worth it.

But the book goes further in an attempt to help those that decide to move forward with a plan to raise equity financing. It provides the entrepreneur with what they must do at a minimum to be prepared to submit a proposal and get through the investment process. Finally, it provides the reader with a basic understanding of the process the investor goes through to reach a decision. Hopefully, this helps the reader understand why the process takes several months, why the investor asks for specific information and why the terms and valuation are what they are. In understanding the Investor's process, constraints and motives, hopefully the entrepreneur will be better prepared to negotiate the terms and work with the investor after they are in the deal.

As the title implies, this guide was written with the entrepreneur as the target reader but there are so many more who should read this book. Those assisting entrepreneurs from public and not for profit small business organizations to coaches, consultants and educators should have this book as a resource for both themselves and those they are attempting to help.

Finally, I hope this guide is more than just something that provides entrepreneurs and others with a basic understanding of early stage equity financing. I hope it is a jumping off point for those that wish to learn even more. That is why in the appendix of this guide there is a resource guide that directs you to useful on-line sites, magazines, organizations and books that can provide other useful information for entrepreneurs and those that work with them.

In summary, here are some of the most critical points to take away from reading this guide:

- A well prepared executive summary and business plan are critical documents to have at the outset of the process

- Financial projections must be integrated and must capture every aspect of the business' operations from staffing and inventory to sales, marketing and accounts receivable.
- While the business plan and financial forecasts get you in the door presentations get you to the next stage. Know your audience and the length of time available. Prepare different presentations for different situations and practice, practice, practice.
- Management is key. If you don't have it get it, if you can't afford show how you plan to acquire it after you are funded.
- Don't use the shotgun approach when applying to investors. Find ones that are investing in your region, at the size investment you are requesting and the stage of development that you have reached.
- The process takes time. Don't get frustrated.
- You only get a handful of opportunities at most. Make the best of them.
- Valuations and term sheets are complicated. Get help.
- It's alright to turn down a term sheet but you only get a few chances so if all of them look unreasonable maybe you are being unreasonable.

- Check out the investor. There are good ones and bad ones. There are ones that are compatible with you and ones that are not.
- Not all entrepreneurs or businesses should take equity financing even if it's being offered. Make sure you have the right stuff.

Most importantly life is short – make sure you have fun at whatever you do. Good luck.

Appendix A

Investment Opportunity Grade

Investment Opportunity Grade

Grade each item, then grade each category as follows:
A- Excellent B- Good C- Average D- Weak   F- Poor

Management

Rate each position on relevant experience, education and business acumen.

Position titles may vary and some positions may be combined

- **CEO**   __
- **CFO**   __
- **COO**   __
- **VP Marketing**   __
- **VP Sales**   __
- **Rate how the management team works together**   __
- **Other management (Describe)**   __

- **Overall Management Grade**   __

Comments:

Market

- **Overall Market Size** ___
- **Competition (number of competitors, size and quality of product)** ___
- **Is the market declining or expanding?** ___
- **Are the products positioned properly?** ___
- **Rank the sales channel being used or Planned** ___
- **Is the channel or sales force incentivized properly?** ___
- **Other** ___

Overall Management Grade ___

Comments ___

Product

- **Product Superiority compared to competition** ___
- **Is product(s) priced right for market positioning?** ___
- **How strong are the barriers to entry?** ___
- **Is the company a single product company and if so can the product line be easily extended?** ___

(Product section continued)

- **Is the product fully developed and ready to for a full roll out?** ___
- **Are there licenses, approvals, certificates or other regulatory hurdles not yet met?** ___
- **Are critical materials or services readily available from multiple sources?** ___
- **Other** ___

Overall Product Grade ___

Comments

Accounting and Financial

- **Are projections realistic and do they tie back to raw data and other reports?** ___
- **Are projections built from the bottom up?** ___
- **Are gross and net margins attractive?** ___
- **Are the accounting functions adequately separated among staff?** ___
- **Are generally accepted accounting practices used?** ___
- **Are periodic accounting reports prepared in a timely manner?** ___
- **Are policies and systems in place for travel and entertainment, overtime, vacation and etc.?** ___

(Accounting and Financial section continued)

- **Are withholding taxes paid current?** ___
- **How well does the company collect Receivables** ___
- **Is the company on C.O.D. with any suppliers, are payables overdue?** ___
- **Other** ___

Overall Accounting and Financial Grade ___

Comments

Operations

(Not all operations items may be applicable to all businesses)

- **Are facilities adequate for next few years' projected growth?** ___
- **Does product flow through the facility look reasonable?** ___
- **Is product distribution well planned and implemented?** ___
- **Is equipment kept in good condition and reasonably new?** ___
- **Is there an equipment replacement program if equipment replacement is a significant cost?** ___
- **Is customer and product service adequately addressed?** ___
- **Other** ___

(Operations section continued)

Overall Operations Grade ___

Comments

Overall Score ___
(This is not an average for some things are weighted higher than others. Rather it is more
subjective after reviewing strengths and weaknesses.)

Comments

Recommendations

Appendix B

Sample Term Sheet

December 18, 2010

John Doe, CEO
XYZ Corp
Peoria, IL 61606

Dear John:

Thank you for allowing ABC Ventures, L.P. the opportunity to consider an investment in your company. Please find below a term sheet for a possible investment by ABC Ventures L.P. in XYZ Corp.

This Term Sheet dated December 18, 2007, summarizes the principal terms of an equity investment (the Investment Transaction) in XYZ Corp. (the "Company") by ABC Ventures, L.P., a Delaware limited partnership (the "Investor"). The terms and conditions in this term sheet including its existence shall be confidential information and shall not be disclosed to any third party. The Transaction shall not be consummated and the obligations relating to the Transaction shall not be enforceable until the documents contemplated by and related to this term sheet are agreed upon, put in final form and executed by the Company and the Investor.

Our proposal is based on projections and information that the Company has provided to us to date. To date the Investor has performed little or no due diligence. Our proposal remains subject to, among other things: (i) completion of business, accounting, and legal due diligence to the satisfaction of ABC; (ii) the negotiation and completion of satisfactory legal documentation relating to our investment, and; (iii) the formal approval of ABC's Investment Committee.

<u>XYZ Corp Transaction is to be Consummated on the Following Terms:</u>

Amount of Investment:	$2,000,000 out of a minimum of $3.0 million and a maximum of $3.25 million Series B offering, provided that other commitments for purchase of Series B stock be made prior to February 29, 2008.
Type of Security:	Series B Preferred Stock, $0.01 par value per share ("Series A Preferred"), convertible into shares of the Company's Common Stock ("Common").
Price Per Share:	$5.00
Investor:	ABC Ventures, L.P. ("ABC" or "Series B Investor").
Shares Purchased:	450,000 shares of Series B Preferred
Type of Security:	Series B Participating Convertible Preferred stock (the "Series Preferred").
Valuation:	$5.3 million pre-money valuation on a fully diluted basis.
Capitalization:	XYZ Corp's current capitalization table, including pro forma adjustments for the issuance of Series B Preferred, is attached as Exhibit A.
Closing:	The closing of the transaction, if all conditions are met, is expected to occur on or before January 31, 2008.
Initial Use of Proceeds:	Working capital and general corporate purposes.

Board of Directors:	The Board of Directors shall be composed of five (5) directors as follows: two Directors to be selected by the Series B Preferred shareholders and three Directors to be selected by the common shareholders.
Dividends:	The series B Preferred will accrue cumulative quarterly dividends at a rate of 8.0% per annum. XYZ Corp., Inc. may not pay any dividend on any other shares until the accrued but unpaid dividends on the Series B Preferred are paid.
Redemption:	Subject to any legal restrictions on the Company's redemption of shares, beginning on the fourth anniversary of the Closing Date, the holders of Series B Preferred may require the Company to redeem all of the outstanding Series B Preferred shares. The redemption price shall be the Purchase Price plus any accrued but unpaid dividends.
Conversion:	The Series B Investors may elect to convert Series B Preferred into common stock at any time. The initial share conversion rate shall be one-for-one (1:1). The Series B Preferred shall automatically be converted into common stock upon the closing of a qualified Initial Public Offering of $30 million or more or a sale of XYZ Corp. for a five times (5.0x) multiple on the Series B price after any "Earn-Out."

Liquidation Preference:

In the event of any liquidation, dissolution or winding up of the Company, the Series B Preferred Investor shall be entitled to receive, in   preference to other classes of stock, an amount equal to one times (1.0x) the Purchase Price plus any accrued but unpaid dividends. After the full liquidation preference has been paid to Series B holders and then Series A holders, any remaining funds and assets of the Company shall be distributed pro rata among the holders of the Series B Preferred, Series A Preferred and the common stock on an as converted basis. If the proceeds from the liquidation, dissolution or winding up of the Company are not sufficient to pay the entire liquidation preference to the Series B Investors, the available proceeds will be paid to the Series B Investors.

Anti-Dilution Preference:

The conversion price of the Series A Preferred will be calculated to provide anti-dilution protection on a "full ratchet" basis in the event that additional shares of Company stock are issued for an effective price of less than the purchase price of Series A Preferred. This "full ratchet" adjustment shall apply but not be limited to stock splits, stock dividends and etc., with customary exceptions for issuances upon conversion or exercise of existing outstanding rights, shares issued in connection with institutional debt financing or equipment lease transactions options or shares granted under the Company's Stock Option Plan or other equity incentive plan for the benefit of its employees and approved by the board of directors.

Voting Rights: Each share of Series B Preferred shall carry a number of votes equal to the number of shares of common stock then issuable upon its conversion. On an "as converted basis," the Series B shall generally vote together with the common stock and not as a separate class except as provided below.

Protective Provisions: The Company shall be required to obtain an affirmative vote of the Series B Preferred shares prior to the Company taking any of the following actions: (a) repurchase or redemption of any shares by the Company or any subsidiary; (b) alter or change the rights, preferences or privileges of the Series B Preferred, including any amendments to the Articles of Incorporation affecting Series B Preferred rights and privileges or documentation; (c) authorize or issue shares of any class of stock having preference or priority as to dividends or assets superior to, or on parity with the Series B Preferred; (d) increase the authorized number of shares of Series B Preferred; (e) increase the number of Company

Directors; or, (f) any sale, merger or consolidation of the Company, (g) the liquidation or dissolution of the Company, or (h) the declaration or payment of a dividend on the stock.

Preemptive Rights: The Series B Investors will have the right to purchase up to its pro rata share of any equity securities offered by the Company on the same price and terms as the Company offers such securities to other potential investors, subject to customary exceptions.

Right of First Refusal: The Series B Investors will have the right to purchase any Common or Preferred shares offered by shareholders of the Company on the same price and terms as such securities are offered to third parties.

Co-Sale Agreement: The holders of Series B Preferred will have the right to participate on a *pari passu* basis with any other shareholder in sales of common or preferred shares to third parties.

Registration Rights: There shall be no demand registration rights prior to a qualified initial public stock offering. Holders of the Series B Preferred shares shall have two free demand registrations beginning six months after the date of a qualified IPO; and unlimited free piggyback registrations and S-3 registrations once the Company qualifies for use of such form of resale. The cost of these offerings, including one counsel for the selling shareholders and excluding underwriters' discounts and commissions, will be borne by the Company.

Exclusivity:

ABC Ventures, L.P. shall be given the exclusive right to invest $2.0 million for a period ending January 31, 2007 by which time the Investor will complete its due diligence and document the investment in a definitive agreement. ABC Ventures, L.P. understands that an additional $1,250,000 of Series B Preferred stock is available for other investors including those that may have already purchased Series B stock.

Fees and Expenses:

The Company will pay all of ABC's legal fees and due diligence expenses reasonably incurred in connection with the preparation negotiation and closing of the investment.

Conditions to Closing:

Any commitment to provide any investment as discussed herein will be subject to terms and conditions as are standard or customary for transactions of this type, all to be satisfactory to the Investor in its sole discretion, including, but not limited to, the following:

(1) Completion of due diligence investigation satisfactory to ABC in its sole discretion.

(2) Purchase Agreement, a Shareholders Agreement that includes but is not limited to the provisions outlined under "Shareholders Agreement" above and related agreements satisfactory to the Investor and the Company, each in their sole discretion.

(3) As of the closing there has been: (i) no material adverse change in the business, operations, financial conditions or prospects of the Company; (ii) no litigation threatened or commenced, which if successful, would challenge the transaction(s) contemplated herein; and, (iii) no material increase in liabilities, liquidated or contingent, and no material decrease in assets of the Company.

(4) The Company's Board and Shareholders shall have acted, as required, to create this new series B Preferred Stock and will have authorized sufficient shares of Series B Preferred, and sufficient Common Stock for its conversion, to effect this transaction.

Please understand that this letter is not to be considered a commitment by ABC but rather is our statement of interest to effect the proposed transaction in accordance with terms and subject to conditions outlined above. Except for the last sentence of this paragraph, this letter should not be construed as a binding agreement on the part of any of the parties. If the terms as outlined herein are satisfactory, please acknowledge the acceptance of such by signing the acknowledgement below and returning this signed letter to our offices no later than 4:00 p.m. CDT, Friday, December 28, 2007.

By signing below, you agree to treat this letter and its contents as being highly confidential and agree not to disclose any of its contents to any persons other than the companies' officers, directors and previously identified advisors.

Sincerely,

ABC Ventures, L.P.

_____

Jude T. Conway, Partner

ACCEPTED AND AGREED TO:

XYZ Corp.

_____

John Doe
Its_____
Date_____

Appendix C

Due Diligence Checklist

Due Diligence Checklist

OWNERSHIP
- List all current owners of the Company's common and preferred stock.
- Classes of stock currently authorized.
- Number of shares authorized in each class.
- List of shareholders and number of shares and class of stock owned.
- Outstanding options, warrants, stock subscriptions or other stock agreements.
- Pledges of shares, if any.

CORPORATE RECORDS
- List of the current directors of the Company – names, address, telephone, e-mail.
- Copy of the Articles of Incorporation and any amendments thereto.
- Minutes of companies By-Laws and any amendments thereto.
- Minutes of stockholders' meetings, including those of any predecessor corporations.
- Minutes of board of directors meetings, including those of any predecessor corporations.
- Minutes of permanent committees of the board, including those of any predecessor corporations.
- Copies of any authorizing resolutions related to any debt or equity financing.
- Summary of business and personal relationships and affiliations among directors, officers, shareholders, creditors, customers, suppliers and other business affiliates of the Company.

CONTRACTS AND COMMITMENTS
- Copies of all material contracts for the Company including, but not limited to, the following:
  - Loan and Credit Agreements

- Mortgages
- Lines of Credit
- Warrants
- Agency or Commission Agreements
- Sales, Marketing and Advertising Agreements
- Insurance Contracts
- Licensing and Royalty Agreements
- Acquisition, Sale or Merger Agreements
- Leases Re; Real Estate, Equipment or Personal Property
- Employment, Termination or Consulting Agreements
- Management Agreements
- Financing, Service and other Agreements with affiliates

- A schedule of the top major suppliers of the Company indicating materials and/or services supplied or purchased; also, copies of any agreements relating to any such suppliers.

- Copies of any loan agreements, line of credit agreements, indentures of other debt instruments (including any guarantees of such loans to another person), and copies of all correspondence related thereto (including, but not limited to, compliance letters, notices of default, etc.).

- Debt schedule summarizing short-term and long-term debt and capital lease obligations with original principal balance, debt service obligations, interest rates, outstanding balances and maturity dates.

- All agreements or plans for mergers, consolidations, reorganizations, acquisitions or the purchase or sale of assets or stock involving the Company, or agreements in principle, currently in effect, with respect to mergers, consolidations, reorganizations, acquisitions or the purchase or sale of assets or stock involving the Company.

- All agreements entered into by the Company out of the ordinary course of business, including consulting, development, partnership and joint venture agreements.
- All employment contracts with management and former senior employees, deferred compensation and similar agreements, and all general employment or collective bargaining agreements with employees.

- Agreements not to compete to which the Company is or was (within the last two years) a party.
- All other material contracts not otherwise listed.

INDUSTRY
- A breakdown sales volume and operating profit.
- New products/service development programs.
- Factors which may impact costs and impair future growth.

MARKETS AND COMPETITION
- Statistical information available on the market (e.g., trade associations, government reports, etc.).
- List of all competitors (name, size and projected market position).
- List of customers that account for more than 5% of sales volume.
- Payment history with significant customers and explain current and future payment procedures.

MARKETING, SALES AND DISTRIBUTION
- Describe marketing and sales organization by service or product and by geographic market.
- Copies of any marketing studies.
- Any formalized plans for expanding markets or increasing market share.

- List significant customer contracts.

- List major customers recently lost by the Company and reasons for loss.

- Discuss pricing strategies, flexibility in pricing and ability to pass costs to customers.

- Credit policies, receivables and collections (economic strength of customers).

OPERATIONS/PRODUCTION

- Describe any production bottlenecks or critical operations.

- Lead times, shipping, projecting production

- Existing capacity (volume and sales) and utilization rates of facilities.

- Provide a list of major suppliers, alternate sources of supply, contract terms and other critical items.

- Current customer order list and backlog.

- Discuss expansion plans, including capacity additions and related expenditures.

- Provide list of any material permits necessary for operation of business.

- Discuss any safety problems the Company has experienced.

FACILITIES AND EQUIPMENT

- Discuss present condition of all facilities, including machinery and equipment.

- Provide copies of depreciation and amortization schedules.

- Discuss adequacy of facilities and equipment for future needs.

- Discuss property insurance policies and insured values.

MANAGEMENT

- Provide organization chart showing titles and functions.
- Provide copies of employment contracts, including non-compete and confidentiality agreements.
- Provide history of management compensation.
- Verify that both professional and personal references of key management have been contacted and that a summary of conversations with references or letters of reference are available for review.
- Verify that personal credit checks and if applicable, background checks have been conducted.
- Verify that any psychological testing conducted as part of due diligence has been completed and a report issued.

INTELLECTUAL PROPERTY

- List of all, patent applications, copyrights, patent licenses and copyright licenses, foreign or domestic, held by the Company.
- List of any trademarks, or service marks registered by the company.
- List any claims of infringement of others intellectual property by the company and any claims by the company against others for intellectual property infringement.
- Provide copies of all agreements involving licensing or acquiring technology, including software, patent, or other technology licenses, or any development or joint-development agreements.
- Provide copies of all agreements where company has licensed or sold any technology to others, including software, patent or other technology licenses.

EMPLOYEES
- Current employee programs (e.g., hiring trends, turnover, training programs, labor shortages).
- List history of labor relations with unions, if any.
- Describe benefit packages, incentive compensation programs.
- Provide a summary of all transactions between the Company and key personnel, including loans, guarantees and contracts with affiliated parties.
- Provide a list of all loans and advances outstanding at the present time by the Company to any officer or director of the Company (including interest rate, security, maturity, and any delinquencies or deficiencies).

TAXES
- Verify that all federal, state and local taxes withheld from wages have been paid current to taxing authorities.
- Verify that income, sales and property taxes are current.

FINANCIAL INFORMATION, PROJECTIONS AND TAXES
- Provide detailed income statements, cash flow statements and balance sheets for all fiscal and recent interim periods (3 to 5 years).
- Provide discussion of recent and projected operating results.
- Provide a copy of strategic plan, if any.
- Provide five year projected income statements, with assumptions.
- Provide detailed capital budget for the next two years.
- Current sales pipeline report for all sales leads.

- All material documents regarding any tax audits or investigations of the Company, and any correspondence with the IRS, or any other taxing authority.
- All documents involving the Company as borrower, lender or guarantor.
- Letters of counsel relating to litigation and other contingent liabilities of the Company.
- List of any off-balance sheet financing activities.

LITIGATION

- Provide a schedule of all pending or threatened legal proceedings (including any arbitration proceedings) to which the Company is a party, providing a brief description of the following information:
  - Parties;
  - Nature of Proceeding;
  - Date and Method commenced, and
  - Amount of damages and other relief sought
- Provide copies of all pleadings and correspondence relating to all pending or threatened litigation or claims involving the Company as plaintiff or defendant.
- Provide a list of names and addresses of all legal counsel that are currently acting, or in the last two years have acted, on behalf of the Company.
- Any file concerning pending or threatened litigation or administrative proceedings, inquiries, or investigations involving the Company or its agents.
- All information concerning any significant claim asserted or threatened by any taxing authority against the Company or other entity for whose taxes the Company could be liable.
- All opinions by counsel to the Company as to any pending litigation against the Company (including letters to auditors).

GOVERNMENTAL REGULATIONS AND FILINGS

- Provide a list or copies of all licenses, permits, consents, authorizations, registrations, from, with, or to any federal, state, or local governmental authority relating to the Company.
- Provide copies of all material correspondence, if any, with federal state, local or similar regulatory authorities or agencies which regulates the company.
- Provide any reports, notices or correspondence relating to any violation or infringement by the Company of federal, state or local government regulations (including, but not limited to, OSHA, EEOC, EPA, Workers Compensation, etc.).

ENVIRONMENTAL ISSUES

- List environmental permits, if any, under which the Company's facilities operate.
- Discuss any environmental risks associated with the Company's businesses; whether any existing environmental regulations are being or have been violated and what procedures the Company maintains to ensure environmental compliance.
- Provide copies of all notices and demands of environmental authorities relating to the operations or property of the Company.
- Describe any existing or potential environmental liabilities and their potential magnitude, if applicable.

RESEARCH AND DEVELOPMENT ISSUES

- Describe the R&D requirements of the company.
- Discuss the R&D strategy, key personnel and major activities.

INSURANCE

- Describe all liability coverage, business insurance, key person, and other insurance coverage.
- Discuss any outstanding claims.

Appendix D

Recommended Resources

Recommended Resources

National Associations

Angel Capital Association,
www.angelcapitalassociation.org
Angelsoft, www.angelsoft.net
National Association of Seed and Venture Funds,
www.nasvf.org
National Association of Small Business Investment
Corporations, www.nasbic.org
National Business Incubator Association, www.nbia.org
National Collegiate Inventors and Innovators Alliance,
www.nciia.org
National Venture Capital Association, www.nvca.org

Foundations

Coleman Foundation, Chicago,
www.colemanfoundation.org
Kauffman Foundation, www.kauffman.org

Magazines and Publications

Black Enterprise Magazine
Entrepreneur Magazine
Fast Company Magazine
How to Really Start Your Own Business, (free from
SCORE offices)
Inc. Magazine
Women Entrepreneur Magazine

Articles

"Anatomy of an Investor Term Sheet", Andrew S. Whitman, 2x Consumer Products Growth Partners, http://www.2xpartners.com/index.php?cat=3
"10 Reasons Investors Pass ...And, Ways To Enhance The Odds of Raising Capital",
Andrew S. Whitman, 2x Consumer Products Growth Partners, http://www.2xpartners.com/index.php?cat=3
How to Lose an Investor Before You Finish Speaking", Cynthia Kocialski,
http://cynthiakocialski.com/blog/2010/08/19/how-to-lose-an-investor-before-you-finish-speaking/

Books

Entrepreneurial Finance, Richard L. Smith and Janet Kilholm Smith, Wiley
Due Diligence List, Scott S. Pickard, Writers Club Press

Other Helpful Websites

Entrepreneurial Advisors, Inc. –
www.entrepreneurialadvisorsinc.com
Guerilla Marketing – www.gmarketing.com
David B. Lerner – www.davidblerner.com
Build A Stronger America –
www.buildastrongeramerica.com
Entrepreneurship.org - www.entrepreneurship.org
Lipper Current - www.lippercurrent.com
U.S. Patent and Trademark Office - www.uspto.gov
SBA – www.sba.gov
RUPRI Center for Rural Enterprise,
www.energizingentrepreneurs.org
Heartland Center for Leadership Development,
www.heartlandcenter.info

Glossary

Glossary

Accredited Investor – A legal term used for investors (individuals or organizations) that are allowed to be offered the opportunity to invest in certain financial offerings that may not be extended to unaccredited investors.

Angel Investors – Wealthy individuals (usually accredited investors) that regularly invest in entrepreneurial companies. Amount of investment may range from $25,000- $1 million+.

Angel Networks – Groups of angel investors that work together to hear investment presentations, review deals, conduct due diligence and make investments.

Angel Funds – An investment fund capitalized by a group of angel investors that makes investments in young entrepreneurial companies.

Anti-Dilution Protection – Term sheet provision that is designed to protect the outside investor from the possibility of a lower valuation in subsequent rounds of financing. The most common method of protecting against anti-dilution is a ratchet (see ratchet).

Barriers to Entry – Obstacles in the path of a competitor that make it difficult to enter a market. Common barriers to entry are intellectual property, high funding requirements, stringent licensing provisions, highly skilled employees or long lead times.

Bootstrapping – A term used to define the practice of self financing a business by whatever means is available such as, maxing out credit cards, selling ones car or getting a second home mortgage.

Bridge Financing – Temporary financing to get a business to the next permanent round of financing or to harvesting (see Harvesting).

Business Accelerator or Business Incubator – "Business incubators nurture the development of entrepreneurial companies, helping them survive and grow during the start-up period, when they are most vulnerable. These programs provide their client companies with business support services and resources tailored to young firms. The most common goals of incubation programs are creating jobs in a community, enhancing a community's entrepreneurial climate, retaining businesses in a community, building or accelerating growth in a local industry, and diversifying local economies." Source: National Business Incubation Association

Cap Table or Capitalization Table – A table that shows a company's ownership by class of stock and percentage ownership of each major shareholder. A capitalization table is usually made part of a term sheet and for this purpose ownership is generally shown on a fully diluted basis (see term sheet and fully diluted basis).

Cash Flow – Cash receipts over cash payments for a given period of time. It is a measure of a business' financial health.

Cash Flow Breakeven Analysis – The level of sales that generates operating cash inflows that are sufficient to cover operating cash outflows.

Conditions Precedent – Conditions, generally stated in a term sheet, which must be met before an investment will move forward.

Common Stock – "Securities representing equity ownership in a corporation, providing voting rights, and entitling the holder to a share of the company's success through dividends and/or capital appreciation. In the event of liquidation, common stockholders have rights to a company's assets only after bondholders, other debt holders, and preferred stockholders have been satisfied." Source: Investorwords.com

Corporate Venturing – The act of a corporation making equity investments in young entrepreneurial ventures, many times for strategic reasons.

Co-Sale Agreement – A condition found in term sheets that allows an outside investor the right to sell a pro rata share of its investment at the same terms and price as another when any other investor sells any of its stock, only if the company is still privately held.

Covenants – An action an entrepreneur agrees to perform (affirmative covenant) or not perform (negative covenant) in exchange for receiving an investment.

Demand Registration Rights – The right of a shareholder to force a company to register its shares for later sale to the public.

Discounted Cash Flow – "A valuation method used to estimate the attractiveness of an investment opportunity. Discounted cash flow (DCF) analysis uses future free cash flow projections and discounts them (most often using the weighted average cost of capital) to arrive at a present value, which is used to evaluate the potential for investment." Source: Investopedia.com

Dividends – A portion of a corporation's profits paid to shareholders of some or all classes of stock based on pro rata ownership, either in cash or in additional shares of stock.

Double Bottom Line – A term used to describe an investment made for more than financial reasons. Usually the second reason is social or environmental.

Due Diligence – "The process of assembling and verifying the information related to an investment decision, whether on behalf of others or oneself." Source: Harvey, Michael G. and Robert F. Lusch (see footnote 1)

EbITDA – Earnings before Interest, Taxes, Depreciation and Amortization. It is a rough measure of a company's net operating cash flow.

Early Stage – The stage in a business' life cycle after it has sales revenue but generally before positive cash flow or profitability.

Elevator Pitch – A short presentation to a possible investor, providing only the most critical information to whet the appetite of the listener, generally three to five minutes in duration. The term comes from the time one would have to pitch an idea to someone else during a ride in an elevator.

Employment Agreements – In the context of Entrepreneurial Development, "employment agreement" generally refers to an Executive Employment, Confidentiality, Non-Competition and Non-Solicitation Agreement. It provides for salary, benefits, stock options and severance pay in exchange for employment services by the executive, his/her promise not to compete in a certain geographic area for a specific time period and not to solicit the company's employees to work at another company for the same time. Also the executive generally agrees to keep confidential any company information that is not already in the public domain.

Enterprise Value – An alternative measure to market capitalization of a company's value. It is calculated as equity plus debt, minus cash and cash equivalents. It assumes that a purchaser would need to assume any company debt but would get to pocket any cash.

Exit – An event that allows outside investors the opportunity to their investment into cash or cash equivalents. The three most common exits are the sale of the company or an Initial Public Offering (IPO) or re-capitalization. Synonym: Harvest

Exit Strategy – A strategy implemented to allow for a specific type of exit whether, sale, IPO or re-capitalization.

Fiduciary - A person or organization who looks after assets on another's behalf.

Fiduciary Duty or Fiduciary Responsibility – A fiduciary's legal responsibility to act in the best interest of the person or entity whose assets they are in charge of. A venture capital fund has a fiduciary duty to its investors. A bank has a fiduciary responsibility to its depositors and shareholders.

Financial Acquisition – An acquisition made for purely financial reasons, as opposed to one where strategic reasons play a part.

Financial Distress – A condition where a business is disappointing its investors or creditors due to among other things, violation of covenants, payment defaults or inability to adequately carry out its business strategy.

Financial Forecasting – The act of making predictions on financial performance of a business based on historical and current data.

Financial Modeling - The process by which a firm constructs a financial representation of some, or all, aspects of the firm by performing calculations and making predictions based on the information.

First Mover Advantage – The advantage a company has when it is first to market with a new technology, concept idea, whether or not it has defensible intellectual property.

Gorilla Marketing – The use of unconventional marketing techniques to get maximum results with minimal financial resources.

Harvest or Harvesting – An event that allows an investor to turn that investment into cash or cash equivalents. In other words harvest its return. Synonym: Exit.

Hurdle Rate – The required rate of return in a discounted cash flow analysis above which an investment makes sense and which it does not, or the required rate of return.

Internal Rate of Return - The rate of return that would make the present value of future cash flows plus the final market value of an investment or business opportunity equal the current market price of the investment or opportunity. The internal rate of return is an important calculation used frequently to determine if a given investment is worthwhile.

Initial Public Offering (IPO) - The first sale by a formerly privately held company to the public. The act of going from a privately held company to a publicly traded company.

Intellectual Property – Certain intangible assets namely expressions and ideas that once established are treated in law as tangible assets and as such cannot be used or taken without the holders permission. The most common forms of intellectual property are copyrights, patents, trademarks, and trade secrets.

Letter of Intent – A letter from a prospective investor or investors that expresses its intent to invest in a business as long as certain conditions are met and due diligence is satisfactory. Usually a "letter of intent" is not as detailed as a term sheet. It may precede a term sheet or be used in place of a term sheet.

Leveraged Transactions – Financial transactions where the amount of debt exceeds traditional levels. In order to compensate for this subordinated debt is used along with senior debt and carries a higher coupon rate and equity enhancements or kickers.

Leveraged Buyout – The use of a higher ratio of debt to equity than normal when purchasing a business. A leverage buyout is a type of leveraged transaction.

Liquidation Preference – The order of preference of various equity and debt classes in the event of the liquidation of a business.

Liquidity – The ability to convert an asset, in this case shares of company stock, easily into cash.

Liquidity Event – An event such as an IPO or acquisition that provides liquidity of a company's stock. Closely related to an exit or harvest.

Lock-up Period (IPO) – A period of time in which shareholders with a large proportion of ownership (such as company executives and venture capital firms) are prohibited from selling shares immediately after a company's IPO. IPO lock-ups typically last anywhere from 90 to 180 days after the first day of trading, and are in place to prevent shareholders with a large proportion of ownership from flooding the market and deflating the price.

Management Buy Out (MBO) – The act of all or part of a company's management team acquiring that company.

Mezzanine Financing - A debt instrument with an equity component, either attached warrants or convertibility, typically used to finance the expansion of existing companies. It is generally subordinated to debt provided by senior lenders such as banks. Since mezzanine financing is usually provided to the borrower with little or no collateral on the part of the borrower, this type of financing is aggressively priced with the lender seeking a return in the 20-30% range.

Net Present Value - The present value of an investment's future net cash flows minus the initial investment.

Non-Compete Agreement – An agreement between a company and an employee, usually in management, research or sales that restricts that employee from directly competing with the company in a certain geographical area for a specified period of time. The employee generally agrees to such a restriction in exchange for stock options and/or a severance package. Sometimes the agreement specifies that the employee may also not solicit or recruit other employees to work for his/her new employer (non-solicitation agreement).

Non-Disclosure Agreement (NDA) or Confidentiality Agreement – Contracts between at least two parties that outline confidential material, knowledge, or information that the parties wish to share with each other for specific purposes, but wish to restrict from third parties. The parties agree not to disclose information covered by the agreement.

Ownership on a Fully Diluted Basis – Stock ownership or capitalization of a company after stock options, warrants and convertible debt is added to outstanding shares.

Participating Preferred Stock – An equity instrument that in the event of a liquidity event, including the sale of the company, requires a company to pay the holder the principal amount of its investment or a multiple of its principal amount and then to pay that holder its pro-rata share of the remaining proceeds based on its percentage ownership.

Piggyback Registration Rights - The rights of an investor to register and sell either some or all of its unregistered stock in the event that the company conducts a public offering.

Post Money Valuation – The value of a company's stock based on the price of a new stock issue after the stock has been purchased or the investment made.

Pre-emptive Rights – The right given to existing shareholders to purchase shares of a new issue before it is offered to others.

Pre Money Valuation – The value of a company's stock before an anticipated or proposed investment is made based on the anticipated stock price of the proposed investment.

Preferred Stock – A class of stock that has a preference in liquidation rights and usually dividend distribution over common stock.

Private Placement - Private placements are offerings of equity or debt that institutions or accredited investors may participate in, but which the public at large is generally excluded from.

Private Placement Memorandum - A legal document used to provide prospective investors in a private placement the details about offering including a company's business plan, investment information, risk factors and other pertinent information. Sometimes referred to as a Reg. D offering.

Private Offering – Any of a number of ways to raise capital from private sources as opposed to raising capital in the public markets. One popular type of offering is the Private Placement Memorandum.

Pro-forma (Financial) – Financial statements showing what one may expect to occur in the future as opposed to financial statements that show actual results.

Prospectus – A formal legal document required by the Securities and Exchange Commission that provides information on an investment offered to the public.

Ratchet – A provision found in many term sheets that is designed to protect the institutional investor from dilution in subsequent rounds of financing. There are "full ratchets and "weighted ratchets." If the valuation of a subsequent round is lower than what the investor originally paid, with a "full ratchet" the investor receives additional shares for free so that the average cost per share is the same as the new investor. With a "weighted ratchet" the investor has the ability to acquire additional shares such that the cost per share is the same as the weighted average price of subsequently issued shares. Source: Smith and Smith, 2004

Redemption Features – Features in a term sheet that allow an investor to redeem its shares for cash at some period in the future, usually at the original purchase price plus market rate interest.

Right of First Refusal – The right of an investor to purchase stock before it is offered to others.

Re-capitalization – Where new investors buy out the original institutional investors, providing them an exit. This is usually a later stage private equity fund purchasing the shares of an earlier stage venture capital fund.

Roll-up IPO – A process where two or more companies are merged for the primary purpose of an initial public offering. See Initial Public Offering.

Royalty – A payment made to the holder of intellectual property for the use of that property usually memorialized in a license agreement. Royalties are usually based on a percentage of sales.

Sales Cycle – The average length of time it takes from first contact with a potential customer to the execution of a sale.

Scenario Analysis – The use of different scenarios when developing financial projections in order to better anticipate and correct discrepancies between projections and actual results. Many times scenarios are expressed as best case, worst case and most likely.

Seed Capital – Equity capital for businesses that are in the earliest stages of development, well before product revenue is generated.

Seed Stage – The earliest stage of development in a company's life cycle when the product or service is at the concept stage, except that some definitions of business life cycle include a pre-seed stage.

Sensitivity Analysis – The practice of changing critical variables in financial projections up or down to assess the impact of those variables on the company's future performance.

Shareholders Agreement – An agreement between shareholders that sets out the parameters of an investment including but not limited to voting rights, liquidation rights, dividend distribution and covenant protection.

Small Business Investment Company (SBIC) – A type of loan or equity fund where the Small Business Administration (SBA) participates as an investor or lender in the fund. Most SBICs tend to be later stage due to the structure of SBA's investment. Many provide a combination of debt and equity or debt with equity enhancements to their portfolio companies.

Start-up – In venture capital terms, the stage in a company's life cycle when a it is ready to generate product revenue. In technology companies this is not the same as the starting date of the company's operations.

Staged Financing – Refers to an investment where the total amount is committed at the outset but where the money is doled out in stages over time based on the company's performance of pre-determined milestones.

Stage of Development – A set of terms used in investment circles to describe the stage of a company in its life cycle. The set of terms generally include the following stages but may not be limited to these stages: seed, start-up, early, growth or expansion, and later stage.

Strategic Acquisition – An acquisition made where financial considerations are not the sole determinant of value. For instance, one food company purchasing another at least partly for product line extension.

Sunk Costs – A sunk cost is a fixed cost that is not recoverable if the project or business is terminated. Not all fixed costs are sunk costs.

Syndication – The process of several investors teaming up to invest as a group in one investment or the investor group itself.

Technology License – A license to use another's intellectual property in exchange for monetary consideration usually in the form of a royalty stream.

Technology Transfer – The act of transferring technology from a research institution, such as a university or laboratory to a commercial enterprise in exchange for monetary consideration, usually in the form of a royalty stream.

Terminal Value – The valuation of a business where existing investments could be reasonably sold to others (terminated) without undue difficulty. It does not imply that the investment will be sold at this time only that it could reasonably be sold. It has nothing to do with the value of a business when it ceases operations.

Term Sheet – A document that summarizes the details of an investment proposal usually by a venture capital firm that is used to prepare final investment agreements.

Turnaround Financing – A specific category of financing provided for companies that are in distress. It is characterized by aggressive pricing and tight financial controls.

Warrant or Detachable Warrant - A security, with an attached derivative giving the holder the right to purchase shares of the underlying security at a specified price at some specified future date.

Working Capital – Current assets minus current liabilities. It measures the amount of liquid assets available to a business to facilitate growth.

Valuation – The act of determining the monetary value of a business or a specific investment in a business.

Venture Capital Fund – A professionally managed fund raised primarily from institutional investors e.g. pension funds, banks, foundations and university endowments. Nearly all venture capital funds are organized as limited partnerships with a ten year life. Venture capital is invested in the form of equity, usually preferred stock, in privately held companies at various stages of development.

Vet (Vetting) - A thorough review of a project prior to moving forward in the investment process.

ABOUT THE AUTHOR

Jude Conway, is currently President and CEO of Entrepreneurial Advisors, Inc., (EAI), a consulting and training firm for entrepreneurs and those serving entrepreneurs. Prior to founding EAI, Mr. Conway served as either a principal or a partner of three venture capital funds over a twenty year span. During that time he evaluated hundreds of business proposals, managed a portfolio of successful investments, valued dozens of businesses and mentored or advised numerous entrepreneurs.

He has been sent into companies as a turn-around advisor and has liquidated a portfolio of under performing investments. He has served on over a dozen boards of Directors of privately held companies and been involved in numerous industry and community initiatives. He also taught an upper level course in Entrepreneurial Finance for two years at Bradley University.

Mr. Conway has written a number of articles and is a well known speaker on the subjects of early stage investing and entrepreneurship. He currently lives and has his office in the Des Moines, Iowa area. You can visit his company's website at
Http://entrepreneurialadvisorsinc.com.

LaVergne, TN USA
30 January 2011
214551LV00002B/10/P

9 781602 647121